The man who invented
The Third Reich

Stan Lauryssens

'His death was almost a suicide,
a suicide prepared for a long time.'

*The French poet Charles Baudelaire,
commenting upon the death of E.A. Poe*

The History Press

For Karen Mascarenhas

First published in 1999
This edition published in 2010

The History Press
The Mill, Brimscombe Port
Stroud, Gloucestershire, GL5 2QG
www.thehistorypress.co.uk

British Library Cataloguing in Publication Data.
A catalogue record for this book is available from the British Library.

ISBN 978 0 7509 3054 3

Typesetting and origination by The History Press
Printed in Great Britain
Manufacturing managed by Jellyfish Print Solutions Ltd

Contents

Acknowledgements

As a young reporter in the early 1970s, I requested an interview with Arno Breker in Düsseldorf. Breker was Hitler's favourite sculptor. The giant marble-eyed bronzes adorning the Court of Honour of the Reich's Chancellery were his. Arno Breker introduced me to Albert Speer and to Otto Skorzeny, the Nazi daredevil who rescued Mussolini from his Gran Sasso prison hideaway. Albert Speer arranged a meeting with Reinhard Gehlen, Hitler's master spy, and Skorzeny introduced me to Dr Werner Naumann, Goebbels' Secretary of State for Propaganda, who in turn introduced me to Sir Oswald Mosley. I spoke to Mosley twice: in his suite at London's Ritz Hotel and over lunch at his palatial residence near Paris, *Le Temple de la Gloire.* The British fascist leader introduced me to Otto Günsche, Hitler's SS bodyguard, and to Otto Strasser who was, at the time, labelled an 'anti-Hitler Nazi'. I listened, observed, and recorded their secret stories. Although they have all passed away, I want to thank them posthumously for sharing their experiences with me. Otto Strasser was the first to mention the man who invented the Third Reich. If I hadn't requested and obtained an interview with Hitler's favourite sculptor, I wouldn't have had lunch with Oswald Mosley, and I would never have met Otto Strasser. In short, it would have been impossible for me to write this book almost 30 years later.

All translations from the German are my own. My thanks are due to the Wiener Library in London for their unfailing and courteous assistance.

Photographs are selected from the following sources: Max Beckmann-Archiv/Bayerische Staatsgemäldesammlungen, Bundesarchiv Koblenz, *Illustrated London News*, Munch Museum, Staatsbibliothek zu Berlin Bildarchiv, Ullstein Bilderdienst and Wiener Library.

ONE
Vienna

Austria is the land of romance. Yet the world is a sad place, as sad as Vienna is, since the Austrian capital has had to pay a heavy price for the Industrial Revolution. Huge, grey blocks of airless apartments and large, silhouetted houses surround the Westbahnhof railway station. Behind every window, 'room for rent' signs are hanging out. The smell of cooked cabbage and light from kerosene lamps stray out of darkened hallways.

There is another Vienna, too. The Vienna you either love or hate. The Vienna of gallant young officers strolling the boulevards in colourful marine and hussar uniforms. The Vienna of the magnificent Habsburg buildings on the Ring-Strasse, where the music of its gifted native sons Haydn, Mozart, Beethoven, Schubert and the Strauss family's gay, haunting waltzes fill the air; the Vienna of the old emperor riding each day past the warm coffee-houses in his gilded carriage drawn by eight white horses.

In the Café Central on the corner of the Stanch-Alley, Leon Trotsky plays chess and harbours dreams of revolution. People walk around in stiff collars and straw hats, polluting the night air with their cigars. They drink mocha and read the international newspapers. In the Hof Opera, Wagner's *Tristan und Isolde* and *Lohengrin* are performed under the direction of Gustav Mahler. Twice daily, Dr Sigmund Freud, who lives in the Berg-Alley, walks around the Ring-Strasse to purchase his cigars at the little tobacco shop near the Michaeler church across from the Neue Burg. Opposite Dr Freud lives Theodor Herzl, a bearded journalist. He works on a book, *The Jewish State*, in which he details his vision of an impending exodus to Palestine.

Like no other city in the West, Vienna breathes an air of the delicate baroque and the elegant rococo, of a gaiety and a charm that are unique among the capitals of the world. According to a popular contemporary song, angels spend their holidays in Vienna. Beneath the woodland, the hills along the Danube are studded with yellow-green vineyards surrounded by the ever-green Wienerwald (Vienna woods), where the last foothills of the Alps reach the city. Like a pearl in an oyster, Vienna lies in the curve of the hills. In 1873, Vienna had been the setting of a World Exhibition. Thirty-four years on, its population has grown to 2 million and rot and decay are threatening this most prosperous of cities at the heart of Europe. In early morning, the spire of St Stephan's Cathedral is lost in the fog. The cobbled streets of the Jewish sector shine with dew.

In the summer of 1907, a provincial dandy from Linz fails the entrance examination of the painting school at the Vienna Academy of Fine Arts. His sample drawings of country landscapes with farms and bridges are not good enough. The judgement of the examiners is recorded in the Classification List for the years 1905 to 1911: 'Sample drawings inadequate'. Rejected by the academy, he wants to become a story writer. He dresses in a dark overcoat and a hat, and carries an ivory-tipped walking stick. The young man from Linz lives in a single unheated back room in the Stumper-Alley 29, up two flights, across the street from the Westbahnhof that accommodates the fast trains from Munich and Paris. He pays a monthly rent of 10 crowns. Since he is an orphan, an Austrian law dating from 1896 entitles him to a monthly government pension of 25 crowns. A small inheritance paid in instalments from the money obtained from the sale of the Leonding family house brings him an extra 17 crowns a month. He spends his time reading, attending political disputes and browsing through the local newspapers. The books he reads are on historical, philosophical and political matters. He skips through the material and takes out those parts that are useful to him. He reads not to learn but in order to find justification for his own feelings and convictions. The book he loves above all others is *Legends of the Gods and Heroes: The Treasures of Germanic Mythology.* For hours, he can pore over it. He has also read *Don Quixote* as well as the Wild West novels about cowboys and Indians, written by Karl May while serving two prison terms for fraud. He frequents the Hofbibliothek where he acquires a copy of *Psychology of Masses*, a famous book by the Frenchman Gustave Le Bon, that has been published in a German translation.

In winter, when the gaslights in the street are lit at 5 p.m. sharp and the young man cannot read any longer, he goes to the Hof Opera at 2 crowns per performance. He secures standing-room in the promenade, directly under the imperial box. Women are not allowed in the promenade. Richard Wagner's music intoxicates and bewitches him. He sees *Lohengrin*, his favourite Wagner opera, at least 10 times. Its hero is a man who seeks the woman who will love him unconditionally. The young man shares his meagre lodgings in the Stumper-Alley with a neighbour friend from Linz named August Kubitzek who finds him hard at work, filling endless pages with his spidery handwriting. Kubitzek asks him what he is writing.

'A play,' the young man replies.

He is also composing an opera, although he has no formal music training; he admits to Kubitzek that he has only taken piano lessons for four months in Linz. The opera is a brutal German myth filled with rape and murder, set in the rugged wastes of Iceland. It deals with the legend of Wieland. He imagines a lake surrounded by flaming volcanoes, icy glaciers and floating Valkyries in shining helmets.

'I will compose the music on the piano,' he explains to his room-mate, 'and you will write down the notes.'

He neither smokes nor drinks, and he doesn't seem to have anything to do with women. Strong, staring eyes dominate his face. His mother's picture hangs over his bed. He has arrived in Vienna with a suitcase full of clothes, in the hope of becoming 'something', but in no circumstances does he want to be a civil servant as his father has been.

He is 18 years of age; his name is Adolf Hitler.

In the famous Viennese coffee-houses, the budding artist from Linz reads the papers and stuffs himself full of pastries with exotic sounding names: Powidltatschkerln, Guglhupf, Wuchteln, Millirahmstrudel, Palatschinken, Mohnbeigerl; the Viennese say their pastries taste like a poem. He does not agree with the common provincial opinion on what art should or should not be. His rejection by the Academy of Fine Arts has instilled in him a hate for 'academic' painting. He begins to take notice of architecture as a 'misunderstood' art form and toys with the idea of becoming a famous architect himself instead of a painter, a composer or a writer. He knows the history of the Viennese buildings in the Ring-Strasse intimately and studies their floor plans; he is interested in all aspects of their construction.

The Ring-Strasse has been created from the leftovers of the old city walls that were built as a defence against the Turks. After Emperor Franz Jozef I ordered the renaissance fortifications and bastions to be demolished, an international competition was established in order to have the area redesigned. On the woodland surrounding the town, houses were built. The Emperor demanded that the capital be made 'bigger and more beautiful'. A final design was approved by the monarch in 1859.

The first representative building to go up was the Hof Opera, in a style referred to as 'classical and late historicism'. Architects brought in from all over Europe transformed the Ring-Strasse into one of the most famous boulevards of Europe, in which symbolism is preferred over function. There is the neo-gothic Rathaus (the City Hall), the Hellenic-columned Parliament, the neo-baroque Imperial Palace in which there are no toilets for the men and women who live and work there, and the Burg Theatre. The Viennese jokingly say that in Parliament you can hear nothing, in the Rathaus you can see nothing, and in the Burg Theatre because of bad acoustics and even worse construction work you can neither hear nor see anything. The balustrades of Parliament are adorned by 60 marble figures of ancient Greek and Roman historians. In front of Parliament, on top of the fountain, stands the statue of Pallas Athene, the goddess of wisdom, wearing a golden helmet and leaning on a gold-tipped spear. The architect of the Hof Opera committed suicide after hearing the emperor's criticism that its steps were too low.

The square across the Ring-Strasse is crowned by the Art Museum and the National History Museum. On one side lies the National Library, on the other the park with its endless flower beds and green gardens. Behind the museums are the Royal Stables which house the emperor's 400 jet-black and snow-white riding horses beneath three vast Bohemian crystal chandeliers. The Heldenplatz (Hero's Square) is the most imperial of squares in all of Europe. Confidentially, the young artist from Linz tells his room-mate that the Heldenplatz would be the perfect setting for mass demonstrations.

Every day at noon, the square is transformed by the military pageantry of the changing of the guard. The Hungarian élite bodyguard rides by, tall and erect on their white horses, dressed in scarlet uniforms trimmed in silver, with sable capes thrown over their shoulders. The old Emperor of Austria and King of Hungary, stooped with age and inevitably dressed in a colourful gala uniform, his mutton-chop sideburns washed and trimmed daily, looks down on the changing of the guard from the window of his office in the Hofburg.

Hitler sketches the new architecture around the Ring-Strasse and visits the Treasure Chamber at the Hofburg where he touches the spear of the Roman centurion Longinus who pierced the side of Christ on the cross. According to legend, whoever claims the spear holds the destiny of the world in his hands. Under grey clouds, he walks to the working-class district of Meidling, where he studies the housing and living conditions of the workmen and their families.

He complains to his room-mate that the dark and dirty tenements have to be swept away to make room for smaller buildings with more conveniences for everyday people. He scrawls sketches of houses with small, detached units of four to eight apartments in which to house the blue-collar workers. He even toys with the idea of a new 'people's drink' to replace wine and beer. His room-mate brings up the question of financing such huge projects.

'Don't worry,' Hitler replies, 'the storm of revolution will take care of that.'

On sunny days, he walks through the rose gardens in the Volksgarten (People's Park) and sips coffee in the Corti'sche Kaffeehaus where Strauss used to give afternoon concerts. Perhaps he has an artist's eye, but he certainly has an artist's temperament. The pungent spice of horse dung that comes from the beautiful blue Danube revolts him. In reality, the Danube is brown and muddy. He is astonished by combustion machines called 'automobiles' of which there are already 300 in Vienna. They claim 60 lives a year. His walking stick clicks on the sidewalk, and the faint melody of Strauss waltzes drifts out of the dancehalls. The young man lives in a dream world. He is looking up at the stars and dreaming new dreams. As happens with dreamers, he is rapidly running out of money. His orphan's pension of 25 crowns per month barely covers his expenses and the inheritance money doesn't come his way any more.

At the National Library, he attempts to get to grips with the cataloguing system. He queues at the visitors' entrance to Parliament and buys a ticket into the public gallery. Inside the semicircular assembly rooms, he sits back and watches the deputies debating and buzzing around in the corridors. Afterwards he sits at his favourite bench in front of the Schönbrunn, under the trees, and reads his papers: the Jewish *Neue Freie Presse* (New Free Press), the *Wiener Tageblatt* (Viennese Daily Paper), the anti-Semitic *Deutsches Volksblatt* (German People's Paper) which he enjoys reading and the Catholic *Das Vaterland* (The Fatherland).

He carries a little notebook in his pocket in which he writes down ideas and makes architectural drawings. In the Prater amusement park, a giant ferris wheel is installed that spins visitors high above the city. In May, when glorious colours and the fragrances of spring burst out from the banks of the Danube, Hitler and his room-mate walk through the Wienerwald to the west of the city, and experiment with water witches trying to find water in the Wienerwald. As money is tight, they live on milk and bread, with a knob of butter on the side of their plates from time to time. Although he hasn't eaten any solid food for days, Hitler writes to Franzl, who lives elsewhere in Vienna, that he is trying to cure himself with a diet of fruit and vegetables after a stomach colic. It is true that he suffers from gastric trouble. He bitterly complains he is living 'a dog's life'.

In 1908, an art show is inaugurated in temporary quarters on a piece of wasteland near the Stadtpark. Gustav Klimt's *The Kiss* is exhibited for the first time. Hitler doesn't like the painting; he says it is a decadent and revolting picture. *The Kiss* is purchased by the Austrian state. As always, Wagner's *Lohengrin* at the Hof Opera is able to cheer him up. One evening he attends a performance of *Tristan und Isolde*; the next day he is among the crowd listening to Wagner's *The Flying Dutchman*. He practises yoga and reads Ibsen, Goethe and the German classics. When his room is infested with cockroaches he gathers them and places them on the end of a straight pin.

August Kubitzek graduates with honours from the Vienna Conservatory of Music and begins a promising professional career as a conductor and composer. On his own again, Hitler moves from Stumper-Alley to a cheaper room at Felber-Strasse 22. He registers his move at the Zentralmeldeamt, the registration office in the Berg-Alley near Dr Sigmund Freud's house. Hitler lists his occupation as 'student'. But in the police records he is referred to as 'a sexual pervert' because most young men from the provinces living in rented accommodation in the city are known to be homosexuals. His hair is growing longer, and the beginnings of a beard go with his flimsy moustache. He increasingly looks like a bohemian artist.

The political mood in Vienna is changing. Politicians are hanging signs over the entrance to their country estates: 'Dogs and Jews forbidden to enter'. The Stock Exchange is nicknamed 'the Jewish Monte Carlo casino'. The socialist mayor of Vienna uses anti-Semitism as a campaign weapon and drugs the crowds with anti-Semitic speeches. Calls are heard for the eradication of the Jews from European culture.

The winter air in Vienna is filled with coal fumes from heating stoves. A new department store has opened its doors, the Gerngross. An eastern European Jew dressed in the traditional caftan is arrested for begging outside the store. Is it a Jew? is the young man's first thought. Or is he a German? He begins to see Jews everywhere.

He eagerly consumes Houston Stewart Chamberlain's

writings which are on sale in every good Vienna bookshop and in the public libraries, and covers the margins with notes. Houston Stewart Chamberlain is an Englishman who lives in Vienna. He has written two books on Wagner and a famous essay in which he attempts to prove that while the Greeks created art and philosophy and the Romans invented the idea of the state and the law, the Jews have had a negative influence on civilization ever since their betrayal of Jesus.

For a few hellers (one heller = a half crown) Hitler buys a copy of the anti-Semitic pamphlet *Ostara*, named after the Germanic goddess of spring. The basic message in *Ostara* is a simple one: the Aryan is a hero by right of blood. The pamphlet is published by Lanz von Liebenfels, an ex-monk who is a member of the Guido von List Society. The society is a blood brotherhood practising medieval black magic; their symbol is the swastika, the solar symbol of millennial Aryan radiance and purity. Members of the Guido von List Society are fascinated by the ancient runic SS letters. They struggle up a hill near Vienna with a knapsack full of empty wine bottles. It is sunrise of the summer solstice and they bury the bottles on the hill in the shape of a swastika to celebrate the longest day of the year. Influential men in all walks of life are members of the Guido von List Society, including the socialist mayor of Vienna. Hitler makes up his mind and joins the Anti-Semite Union of Vienna.

In the back of the Café Central on the corner of Stanch-Alley – where 300 newspapers on cane holders are ringing the walls – sits a man looking younger than his 30 years. He is concentrating on a chess move. He wears a well-clipped moustache, and oval frameless glasses. He is, by all accounts, an intellectual. He has been living permanently in Vienna since 1907, having arrived in the city around the same time as the young painter from Linz. His name is Lev Bronstein but everyone in Vienna knows him as Leon Trotsky. With his second wife and two children, he shares a small villa in the suburb of Sievering. Trotsky writes articles for Russian journals on Viennese art exhibitions and publishes his own Russian-language newspaper in Vienna, called *Pravda*. It is one of the 300 newspapers on cane holders in the Café Central.

Leon Trotsky is not the only revolutionary living in Vienna. In nearby Wiener Neustadt, the 'new Vienna', Tito works as a car mechanic. There is also Lou Andreas-Salomé who has come to Vienna to study under Dr Sigmund Freud. She is a writer and pioneering psychoanalyst who has been a confidante of Nietzsche. She is also the lover of the talented poet Rainer Maria Rilke, who works in Paris himself as private secretary to Rodin, the famous sculptor. One of the stars of the international peace movement lives in Vienna. Her name is Bertha von Suttner, a one-time secretary of Alfred Nobel. She received the Nobel Peace Prize in 1905, as the fifth recipient. Often Rainer Maria Rilke is in town, reading his poetry at the New Vienna Stage. The Austrian expressionist painter Oskar Kokoschka exhibits in Vienna. He is a student of the School of Arts and Crafts. The press calls his exhibition 'the chamber of horrors'. He has arranged four large tapestry designs on the walls, and a series of mad, violent paintings, such as a self-portrait of himself as a young artist: nothing but a skull in blue wash. The painting has been purchased by the modernist architect Adolf Loos. When Archduke Franz Ferdinand remarks in public that he would see no harm in breaking every bone in the artist's body, Oskar Kokoschka moves to the intellectually more tolerant atmosphere of Berlin.

Another expressionist painter hangs himself: Richard Gerstl, who is considered to be 'the Viennese Van Gogh'. His heavy, intense self-expression makes his paintings painful to look at. Gerstl is only 25 when he kills himself. In a Prater café, a man shoots himself in the chest because he has lost his job. Customers quietly sip their mocha, and let the man bleed to death. 'In Vienna, suicide is a way of life,' the newspapers report. Gustav Mahler's musician brother kills himself. The daughter of novelist Arthur Schnitzler dies of blood poisoning after slashing her wrists. The painter Alfred Kubin tries to shoot himself on the grave of his mother.

A major painter on the Viennese art scene makes his début at the 1909 Art Exhibition. His name is Egon Schiele. He exhibits four portraits. The press complains at the obscenity of his pictures. Ludwig Wittgenstein lives in Vienna. He is the ninth child of a rich industrialist. Three of his brothers have committed suicide; all three were homosexuals. His older brother Paul becomes a successful concert pianist after losing his right arm. The French composer Maurice Ravel writes his *Concerto for the left hand* with Wittgenstein's brother Paul in mind.

A Russian named Joseph Dzugashvili gets off the train at Vienna North train station. He calls himself 'Koba' or 'Stalin', a pseudonym. 'Stalin' is Russian for 'man of steel'. Lenin has sent him to Vienna to study life in a city of twelve nationalities. That is the official explanation. Unofficially, Stalin has come to Vienna to spy on his countrymen. On the surface, life in Vienna is pleasant and charming, but deep down Austria is in turmoil. There has been a drastic increase in the cost of living. The price of crude oil used for cooking has gone up 800 per cent in just five years. Spontaneous riots break out. The government calls in the police; when the police fail to restore the calm, the infantry charges with blank sabres. Two protesters are killed. The Minister of Justice is shot at in Parliament. All over the Balkans, the political situation is going from bad to worse. The voices of war are being heard. Soon the world will travel down the road to Sarajevo.

An elegant dandy, dressed in a long, dark rubber raincoat, monocle in the eye, walks along the Ring-Strasse in Vienna, leaning on a walking stick with a silver handgrip. Moeller van den Bruck is a tall, slightly stooped man with sand-coloured hair and a small, well-trimmed moustache. He is 35 years of age. There is an air of melancholy about him, in the way he walks and tilts his head; an air of *Weltschmerz*, of sorrow and sentimental pessimism. Any day now, he will be going home. He has come to Vienna to pay his respects to Houston Stewart Chamberlain, the prolific writer on philosophical and historical subjects. One book in particular has made Chamberlain famous: *The Foundations of the Nineteenth Century*, a revealing and highly romanticized conception of the Germans as the master race with a mission to rule the world. It has passed through eight editions already. Chamberlain is married to Eva Wagner, the composer's daughter.

Moeller van den Bruck walks into the Café Central, orders a mocha, and starts reading the Russian-language *Pravda* newspaper. He sturdily calls himself *ein Augenmensch*; he can steal with his eyes. Moeller van den Bruck is fluent in Russian, as he is in French and English.

Arthur Wilhelm Ernst Victor Moeller van den Bruck was born on 23 April 1876 in a solid bourgeois family on the Kaiser-Strasse 221 in the German town of Solingen in Westphalia, as the only child of state architect Ottomar Victor Moeller and Elise van den Bruck, the daughter of an architect of Dutch origin from Deutz, near Cologne. Contemporary sources describe Elise van den Bruck as 'a stunning beauty'. It is said that her mother was Spanish. Moeller van den Bruck is a native to that Central Saxony which gave birth to the philosopher, writer and mathematician Leibniz and the genial moral philosopher Friedrich Nietzsche, whose life of isolation and illness culminated in madness when he was only 44. Moeller van den Bruck was given the Christian name of 'Arthur' because of his father's adoration for the philosopher Arthur Schopenhauer (1788–1860), the first German philosopher to see the world from an explicitly non-religious viewpoint. Because of professional duties, Ottomar Moeller was transplanted to the Rhineland, where he built the first modern prison in Germany, in Düsseldorf.

Moeller van den Bruck grows up to become a serious and sad young man, who suffers from bouts of melancholy. His schoolfriends are used to saying to each other: 'Did you see? Today he actually *laughed*!' Since his uncles were officers in the Prussian army, Moeller van den Bruck too is destined for a military career; but when he is 20 years of age, he drops the 'Arthur' from his name and moves to Berlin in search of artistic fame. He lives in a villa close to one of the lakes around Berlin, publishes some poetry and even starts writing a novel.

Moeller van den Bruck considers himself to be a nineteenth-century philosophical scholar at the beginning of the twentieth century. He refuses to have his photograph taken; he wants to remain a mystery man. He intends to write a vast encyclopaedia of European values. When both his parents pass away, he comes into a large inheritance. Moeller van den Bruck is free to live the life he pleases. He becomes a dandy and a dreamer; his vestimentary model is Beau Brummel, the Englishman who set the fashion in men's clothes in the first half of the nineteenth century.

In a Berlin wine cellar nicknamed 'Zum Schwarzen Ferkel' (At the Black Piglet) he meets the Norwegian painter Edvard Munch, and they become close friends. A hostile reception to his exhibitions in Kristiana, as Oslo has been renamed, and an unhappy love affair with a red-haired woman have driven Munch out of his own country. Other friends from that period of Moeller van den Bruck's life are the Finnish writer Adolf Paul, the Polish novelist Stanislaw Przybyszewski, the composer Conrad Ansorge, the anthroposophist Rudolf Steiner, the dramatist Frank Wedekind who has returned from America, and the Swedish dramatist August Strindberg. They are the centre around which a male fraternity of Scandinavian, Polish and German writers, artists and critics gather. Strindberg describes the atmosphere in the 'Schwarzen Ferkel' as 'a collection of damned souls: curses, hatred, windows broken by flying bottles, howls and screeches. Passers-by saying:

"What a hell!"' Heated discussions about women, art and sex dominate the conversations.

During his first stay in Berlin, Munch learns the technique of transfer lithography which enables him to recreate and duplicate his images, beginning with *The Scream*.

The brightest star of the circle of drinking friends is the Polish novelist Przybyszewski. He has written a trilogy novel, *Homo Sapiens*, in which he has mixed the experiences of the Berlin bohemians with fictional events to create a mythology of sexuality, jealousy, violent psychological turmoil, dreams and hallucinations.

Moeller van den Bruck writes a five-page article about Stanislas Przybyszewski that is published in a Leipzig-based monthly dedicated to literature, art and social politics. It is the first time that Moeller van den Bruck sees his name in print at the bottom of an article. He is 20 years of age. He marries Hedda Maase from Düsseldorf. They have known each other since childhood days. Hedda Maase is a professional translator, and together they transcribe the stories of French decadent novelist Jules Barbey d'Aurevilley into German. They are published in three volumes as *Die Besessenen* (The Possessed) in 1900 in a series called 'Classics of World Literature'. With the help of Hedwig Lachmann Landauer, who published a German translation of Oscar Wilde's *Salomé*, Hedda and Moeller van den Bruck translate a German edition of the complete works of Edgar Allan Poe, short stories as well as poems. Hedwig Lachmann Landauer is the wife of the anarcho-socialist Gustav Landauer. The Landauers are neighbours of the painter Max Beckmann, and Beckmann is the first individual to acquire the complete ten-volume Edgar Allan Poe edition. With Barbey d'Aurevilley and

Poe out of the way, Moeller van den Bruck confronts the German translation of *Confessions of an English Opium-Eater* in which Thomas de Quincey (1785–1859) analyses his own progress as a consumer of enormous quantities of opium. The *Confessions* is less about the dangers of addiction and more about the revelations of the subconscious mind in dreams and visions; not the opium-eater, but the opium is the true hero of the tale.

When the book was first published in 1822, the *Confessions of an English Opium-Eater* was nothing short of a sensation. Its black humour and vivid, evocative language influenced many writers, from Baudelaire to Edgar Allan Poe. Thomas de Quincey was born in Manchester in 1785, the second son of a linen merchant. He was educated in Bath, Winkfield and at Manchester Grammar School, but he ran away from the last establishment to wander homeless in Wales and London, experiences which he later recounted in his *Confessions*. He attended Worcester College, Oxford, where in 1804 he first indulged in opium. By 1812 he had become an opium addict. At the time, opium was a legal painkiller. 'What was it that did in reality make me an opium-eater? That affection which finally drove me into the *habitual* use of opium, what was it?' Thomas de Quincey asks himself. 'Pain was it? No, but misery. Casual overcasting of sunshine was it? No, but bleak desolation. Gloom was it that might have departed? No, but settled and abiding darkness.' He adds a phrase of Milton's *Samson Agonistes*: 'Total eclipse, without all hope of day!'

Thomas de Quincey suffered from rheumatism in the face, combined with severe toothache. In his book, he describes the pain as 'lancinating pangs – keen, arrowy radiations of anguish', worse than cancer, as if rats were gnawing at the lining of his stomach. He could have taken 'a trifling dose of colocynth', a drug derived from the unripe but full-grown 'bitter apple' and one of the most effective painkillers known at the time, but the extremity of pain drove him to the use first of lozenges – diamond-shaped pills containing opium and described for the relief of pulmonary affections – then to the stronger laudanum, the tincture of opium. He bought the drug in London's Oxford Street: 'On a Saturday afternoon, the counters of the druggists were strewed with pills of one, two or three grains, in preparation for the known demand of the evening. Three respectable London druggists from whom I happened to be purchasing small quantities of opium assured me that the number of *amateur* opium-eaters who were purchasing it *with a view to suicide* was at this time immense.' He consumed up to 1,000 drops of laudanum per day; 60 are prescribed. Twenty-five drops are equivalent to one grain of opium. 'Arrived at my lodgings,' wrote Thomas de Quincey, 'I lost not a moment in taking the quantity prescribed, and in an hour, O heavens! what a revulsion! what a resurrection, from its lower depths of the inner spirit! what an apocalypse of the world within me!' Under the various stages of opium influence, dreams and noonday visions arose.

The opium – 'this great elixir of resurrection' – enabled Thomas de Quincey to study German metaphysics and the writings of the German philosophers Kant, Fichte and Schelling: 'I read Immanuel Kant again; and again I understood him, or fancied that I did.' In a powerful language, Thomas de Quincey described the revelations of the subconscious mind in dreams and visions, shaped by such diverse influences as his early poverty in the area of London's Oxford Street, his friendship with a prostitute, the loss of a child and the chance visit of a Malay sailor. Thomas de Quincey died in Edinburgh in 1859. Moeller van den Bruck's German edition of Thomas de Quincey's *Confessions of an English Opium-Eater* is published in 1902 in Berlin and Leipzig as *Bekenntnise eines Opium-Essers*. The 'English' has been left out of the German title.

Strindberg elopes to Helgoland. Munch travels with his paintings to Dresden and Munich and then to Paris. Przybyszewski, who had shared his home and his wife with a Russian anarchist, goes to prison on suspicion of having murdered his wife along with her children.

In those few short years in Berlin, Moeller van den Bruck completely squanders his inheritance, while he has started borrowing money as advances on projected translations such as Charles Baudelaire and Guy de Maupassant. Most of the money he has lost at the roulette tables. He vows never to gamble again. Harassed by financial worries and on the run from his creditors, Moeller van den Bruck flees to Paris, leaving his pregnant wife behind in Berlin. He travels by train to Frankfurt, sleeping in a second-class coach, and proceeds by steamer down the Rhine to Cologne, where he boards another train to Paris. Or is there another reason apart from money problems why he chooses to disappear? In a cryptic letter to a family relative, his wife Hedda writes that 'in order to escape the paralysing and life-threatening circumstances which fate has put upon him, my husband Moeller van den Bruck, an innocent victim of his own demons, has left for Paris'.

Poverty-stricken at first, Moeller van den Bruck shares

a flat with the German symbolist poet Franz Evers, who is paying the bills. He is a regular visitor to the Closerie des Lilas, the watering-hole of the German colony in Paris, located at the intersection of the Boulevard du Montparnasse and Boulevard Saint-Michel.

Edvard Munch exhibits eight paintings at the Salon des Indépendants. Since he is repudiated by the Norwegian community in Paris, Moeller van den Bruck welcomes Munch into the German colony. Munch likes to spend his evenings in the Closerie des Lilas in the company of the English violist Eva Mudocci, with whom he has formed a close friendship. She specializes in concerts of Scandinavian music, performed in antique peasant costumes. Munch draws a lithograph of Eva, with her long, flowing black hair loosened over her shoulders. He applies the title *Eva Mudocci (Madonna: The Brooch)* to the work. But his continuing participation in the annual Salon des Indépendants fails to bring significant attention, although essays on his art in the *Mercure de France* and the *Gazette des Beaux-Arts* generate much publicity.

One of the paintings Munch exhibits at the Salon is *La Mort de Marat* (Marat's Death), painted in broad and harsh brushstrokes and dark and bloody tones. It is a frightening painting. Marat is lying on a mattress, naked, his arms outstretched like Christ on the cross, his body covered in blood. Next to the bed stands a naked woman, red-haired, holding a bloodied knife. On a round table is a still life, Cézanne-like.

Moeller van den Bruck argues that the reason for Munch's inability to conquer Paris lies in his Nordic soul. While artistic success eludes them, they find refuge in alcohol, which only aggravates their mental turmoil.

An American doctor sits in the café. 'It will end badly with them,' he says. Moeller van den Bruck is a sad, silent man, occasionally overtaken by bouts of melancholy. He stills his melancholy and deadens the pain in his chest by drinking. His best friend in Paris is the German art dealer Samuel Bing whose new gallery L'Art Nouveau supports the work of the Nabis painters Bonnard and Vuillard. Another German from Berlin drinking chartreuse, absinthe and mortal quantities of red wine in the Closerie des Lilas, is Max Beckmann. He lives down the street and studies models at the Julian and Colarossie academies where artists can work paying an hourly fee.

On 28 January 1904 Max Beckmann, sitting in the Closerie, writes in his small blue diary: 'I come here so often that the waiters are amused. Perhaps partly because we were so drunk yesterday. The air is always the same, the gloom is always the same, and so is the urge to create.' On 2 February: 'The Closerie. Very good red wine. Cigar smoke. Norwegian-speaking. The noble Munch is sitting opposite me. By the way, Closerie des Lilas means lilac gardens, as I recently learned.'

When they are bored with the Closerie des Lilas, they go to the Café Rouge, just north of the Jardin du Luxembourg, that features a variety of popular musical entertainment, from vaudeville and operettas to Schubert's *The Trout Piano Quintet*. Accompanied by Max Beckmann, Moeller van den Bruck visits the 1904 Salon des Indépendants and the Durand-Ruel gallery where paintings by Manet, Renoir, Cézanne and Sisley are exhibited.

Moeller van den Bruck undertakes his projected encyclopaedia of European values and titles it *The Germans*; it turns out to be a series of short literary biographies of leading German luminaries since the beginning of Western civilization, such as Luther, the poet and historian Schiller, Nietzsche and Heinrich von Kleist, among others. 'The nation needs new blood,' Moeller van den Bruck writes. 'The sons have to fight their fathers.' *The Germans* is published in eight volumes. One volume is entirely dedicated to Goethe. Three years after the publication of the first volume only one review, in a children's magazine, has drawn attention to *The Germans*.

The lack of recognition does not dampen Moeller van den Bruck's enthusiasm. The discipline of work is aided by alcohol, and he immediately undertakes to write *Our Contemporaries*, in one volume only. The book is a compilation of short biographies of non-Germans: Houston Stewart Chamberlain, Edvard Munch, August Strindberg, Rodin, the Belgian poet Maurice Maeterlinck, Gorki, the Italian novelist Gabriele d'Annunzio and Theodore Roosevelt. 'Culture is a brainchild,' Moeller van den Bruck writes in his introduction, 'while civilisation is situated somewhere in the region of the stomach.' His painter friend Munch intends to do the same as Moeller van den Bruck in painting a series of portraits of contemporary authors. He will complete only one lithograph portrait, of Strindberg.

Tired with Paris, Moeller van den Bruck longs to escape to America, where a brother of his father is successful in business. It is a dream that will never come true. Moeller van den Bruck is prolific in the extreme. He starts writing *Modern Literature*, a series of short essays on world literature. They are published in twelve volumes.

In December 1902, his son Peter Wolfgang is born. Although Moeller van den Bruck has by now divorced his wife Hedda, she still supports him financially and sends him a small monthly allowance that covers his basic needs.

In the Closerie des Lilas Moeller van den Bruck meets the poet Dimitri Mereschkowski (1865–1941). He is one of the founders of Russian symbolism and has published a prose trilogy entitled *Hristos i Antihrist* (Christ and Antichrist). Mereschkowski is married to Less Kaerrick. She has a sister, Lucy. Repelled by French scepticism, Moeller van den Bruck swings over to Russian mysticism. With the aid and under the inspiration of Mereschkowski and Less Kaerrick, he sets out to work on a translation of the complete works of Fyodor Dostoyevsky. When he was a young man, 15 or so, Mereschkowski met the famous Dostoyevsky, who told the aspiring poet: 'To be a writer, you have to live a life of suffering.' Moeller van den Bruck marries Lucy Kaerrick. Between 1905 and 1922 'the complete Dostoyevsky' – in a translation by Moeller van den Bruck and Less Kaerrick, who uses the pseudonym E.K. Rahsin – is published by Piper-Verlag in Munich, in 22 hardbound volumes. The Dostoyevsky translation is a critical and a commercial success. The first volume to be published is the translation of *The Devils*. Then follows *Crime and Punishment* in which Dostoyevsky tells how Raskolnikov murders an old woman moneylender and her unfortunate sister.

His royalties allow Moeller van den Bruck to return to his beloved and dearly missed Germany, and to face his creditors. He is delighted to be reunited with Germany, German-speaking people and German beer and wine. In Berlin he attends an Esperanto congress. The participants are full of hope of future universal human understanding and compassion. But like Goethe and Nietzsche before him, Moeller van den Bruck feels the allure of the Mediterranean, and in 1906 he crosses the border into Italy for the first time in his life. With two German friends, the poet Theodor Däubler (1876–1934) and the expressionist sculptor Ernst Barlach (1870–1938), Moeller van den Bruck and his second wife Lucy live for a year in Florence, in the heart of the Tuscany hills, staying at the Villa Romana which has been newly acquired by the German Artists' League. Max Beckmann intends to join his friends in Italy, but once he has arrived in Geneva he abandons his Italian plans and instead returns to Berlin.

With Däubler, Moeller van den Bruck undertakes the writing of the epic poem *Northern Lights*. The poem is published in 1910 and consists of 30,000 verses. *Northern Lights* is the epic tale of a mythical time when the earth was united with the sun. The earth is the feminine ideal while the sun is the masculine and spiritual principle. All existence is a 'return to the sun' and all creativity has its source in the male principle.

In 1908 Moeller van den Bruck travels to England. He will try to buy the German translation rights of Daniel Defoe's *Moll Flanders*. In 1909 he is in Paris again, where he acquires the translation rights to Guy de Maupassant's short stories. He spends some time sun-worshipping on the isle of Sicily before criss-crossing Russia, Finland, Denmark and Sweden. Moeller van den Bruck lives the bohemian life of the successful artist. In 1911 he finally arrives in Vienna, where he will stay for another year.

Adolf Hitler is queuing for soup at the Sisters of Mercy. The dandy in him is gone; gone are the good suit and the ivory-tipped walking stick. They have gone the same way as his hat and overcoat: to the pawnbroker. He is rapidly running out of money, and accepts a job as a construction worker. After a couple of weeks, he is fired. He moves into the cheapest room in a block of flats at Sechshauser-Strasse 58 (Six Houses Street) and files the customary moving slip with the police. This time, he does not register as a 'student' but as a 'writer', although he hasn't published anything yet. When he fails to pay his rent, he is thrown out. Poverty can be a full-time job, especially in the heart of a Viennese winter. Hitler wanders across the city from shelter to shelter for a bowl of soup and some sleep. He is reluctant to eat in the cheap university canteen because Jews are always present. He has to fill in forms and registration slips in order to be admitted to the kitchens of civic shelters and to the warmth of temporary asylums. He takes weekly showers at the Meidling Asylum run by the Association for Shelter of the Homeless; they disinfect and bleach out his clothes. For a few *groschen*, he hires a bed for a couple of hours at a time. He lives a miserable life, and has to use his school certificate as toilet paper.

Hitler is not alone in his misery: 5 per cent of Vienna's population live on handouts. More than a million servings of soup and shelter are provided yearly at so-called 'warming rooms' where smoking and talking are forbidden, and bodies packed onto wooden benches jerk back and forth in frustrated sleep. Those who do not find a place to sleep in a warming room make their way to the sewers which run parallel with the Danube canal and the River Wien. The moist, damp vapour of the sewage canals cuts through the winter chill. There are out-of-work professors, industrialists who have fallen on hard times and noblemen among the homeless. Hitler tries his luck as a porter at the Westbahnhof railway station, and as a snow shoveller. Despite his miserable frame of mind, he clings to his aesthetic ambitions and queues in bitter weather for the cheapest opera tickets. When it gets freezing cold, he seeks warmth in some Viennese museums.

A friend from the soup kitchens finds him a new residence at 25 Meldemann-Strasse, in a men's hostel that resembles a big hotel, equipped as it is with a dining-room, writing-room and library. He devours the library books. Hitler pays for his stay in the men's hostel by selling little postcard scenes of Viennese architecture done in watercolour, and living off a small inheritance from his mother's sister. His postcard views of Vienna are mainly copied from photographs. He also makes some larger paintings on paper two to three times the size of a postcard. A friend sells them to picture dealers and frame manufacturers. Although he receives only modest sums for his sketches, watercolour paintings and postcard images, they yield a small and fairly regular income. Sometimes one of his original pen-and-ink drawings brings in as much as 10 crowns. As soon as he has sold a picture and has some money in his pocket, Hitler stops painting and listens to the discussions in Parliament, reads the newspapers in coffee-houses and participates in political debating. It makes him angry that several of the politicians in the Viennese Parliament do not speak German at all, but their native Slavic languages.

Everything from religion to socialism is discussed among the homeless at the men's hostel. Many years later, Hitler will proudly recall: 'At that time, I formed a view of life which became the granite foundation of all my actions.' He picks up a pamphlet entitled *Handbook of the Jewish Question*, written by a Viennese named Theodor Fritsch. The publisher describes it as 'a guide to anti-Semitism'. The pamphlet is a collection of anti-Semitic quotes from Erasmus and Voltaire to Wagner, and intends to prove that the Jews are conspiring with the Freemasons to seize world power.

On every street corner, notices are posted reminding the age group born in 1889 to register for military service. Hitler ignores the notices. He is tired of Vienna and spends some time walking in the countryside by himself. On one of his walks, he stops behind the General Hospital and listens to the wailing of the lunatics in the Fool's Tower. He turns 24 and has become, in his own words, 'a friendly and charming person, good of heart and helpful'. He would love to enter the Munich Art Academy in order to become a famous architect. The time has come to leave Vienna, and Hitler boards a train in the same Westbahnhof railway station where he first arrived six years earlier. 'I set foot in Vienna still half a boy, and I will leave the city as a man,' he muses.

Two days later, he is in Munich, in the company of Rudolf Häusler, a friend from the men's hostel. Another country where the same language is spoken. Hitler falsely registers with the Munich police as stateless and gives his address as Schleissheimer-Strasse 34, third floor, in a boarding-house in a poor section of the city run by a tailor named Josef Popp. Hitler shares his flat with his friend Häusler. He gives his profession as painter and writer. Hitler loves the beer halls of Munich as much as he loved the coffee-houses of Vienna. Walking around Munich, he notices that the best-selling hardback in the Munich bookshops is a political tract written by a German with an Italian-sounding name: Friedrich von Bernhardi. Its title says it all: *Germany and the Next War.* The author argues that a preventive war against the Western powers is the only way to save German culture from being overwhelmed by France, Britain and Russia. Hitler immediately buys the book and devours it, fascinated.

Twelve years previously, a balding Russian emigrant lived in the Schleissheimer-Strasse 106, first floor, at the other end of the street from where Hitler lives. His name was Vladimir Ilyich Ulyanov, but he called himself Lenin.

TWO

The Music of War

Since 1910, when he was 21, Adolf Hitler had been subject to military service, but the Austrian authorities could not put their finger on him while he was in Vienna, although he had regularly reported to the police. He ignores a third and final order to present himself for military service, because he does not want to serve in the Austrian army. He loathes the idea of being enlisted in the same ranks with Jews, Slavs and some of the other minority races of the Austrian Empire. The authorities finally locate Hitler in Munich and order him to report for medical examination in Linz where he spent his childhood days. He writes a letter of apology to the military services in Austria in which he requests to be allowed to take his medical examination in Salzburg, on the pretext that he lacks the funds to travel all the way to Linz. Salzburg is nearer to Munich than Linz. Adolf Hitler is examined in Salzburg and is found to be unfit for military service in the Austrian army due to poor health.

In Berlin, the young expressionist painter Max Beckmann announces his intention to paint the gods and heroes of his age when, during the night of 14/15 April 1912, the largest and most modern luxury liner in the world sinks on its maiden trip in a calm sea after colliding with an iceberg. Reading about the catastrophe in his Berlin newspaper, Max Beckmann immediately decides to attempt a painting. He notes in his diary: 'Worked like mad on the *Titanic* for another ten days.' With great pathos and in dark, sad colours, Beckmann expresses the disaster caused by failure 'of a false titan, the machine'. He entitles his painting *Sinking of the 'Titanic'*.

Soon after it is finished, he gives it a key place in an arrangement he has set up in his studio on behalf of a photographer friend. To the artist's right, leaning against the wall, is the *Large Death Scene* of 1906, a painting still Impressionist in style in which the artist mourns the death of his mother. At the left in the photograph is a painting of a female nude, and further left stands an empty easel, draped with the artist's hat and coat. Max Beckmann is seated before the lower right corner of *Sinking of the 'Titanic'*, at the very point in the painting where a drowning man is attempting to clamber into an already overcrowded lifeboat. The journalist who visits the studio sees in the nude on the left a symbol of birth or the beginning of life, the *Titanic*'s disaster as life's struggle and the body on the deathbed as a symbol for the end of life.

When *Sinking of the 'Titanic'* is exhibited at the Berlin Secession show in spring 1913 – the city's major exhibition space for modern art housed in a building on the Kurfürstendamm – the huge canvas enrages the critics. Max Beckmann is bluntly told that his painting lacks the pathos and hope of salvation that makes Géricault's *Raft of the 'Medusa'* an authentic masterpiece. One critic says that Beckmann's canvas might serve for a film poster, but that it is certainly out of place in a serious art exhibition.

For two days over Easter, on 12 and 13 April 1914, Franz Kafka is in Berlin. He stays in a hostel, the Askanischen

Hof in the Königgrätzer-Strasse, and intends to visit Felice Bauer, a young woman from Berlin whom he met two years previously at the home of Max Brod. Felice Bauer works for the Carl Lindström parlophone company in Berlin. For the past two years, Kafka has written to her up to three times a day. Two nights after his first letter to Felice, he wrote his short story *The Judgement* during a single night, in ten hours. He dedicated the story to Felice Bauer, but she doesn't like Kafka's literary prose. She prefers to read Else Lasker-Schüler, Selma Lagerlöf, Franz Werfel, Arthur Schnitzler and Herbert Eulenberg. Kafka calls the poet Else Lasker-Schüler 'a drunk roaming the streets at night'. Felice is particularly enthusiastic about Herbert Eulenberg. Kafka belittles the dramatist, saying he is 'mediocre and below average'.

The Sunday before Easter 1914, Kafka writes to Felice: 'Would you have any one hour to spare for me?' On Monday he writes: 'I don't know if I shall be able to come.' On Tuesday: 'I could come.' On Wednesday: 'I am going to Berlin for no other reason than to show you who I really am.' On Thursday: 'Possible obstacles to my short journey.' On Friday: 'It's not yet at all certain that I'll come.' On Saturday: 'Still undecided.' The same day, he catches the train to Berlin and arrives there late in the evening. On Easter Sunday Kafka writes from the Askanischen Hof: 'What has happened Felice? Now I am in Berlin, and no word from you.' They meet, but for a few moments only. It is their first meeting in more than seven months. On a walk in the Tiergarten Zoo, Kafka humbles himself before Felice 'like a dog' but achieves nothing. Yet he agrees to get engaged to be married, although immediately he regrets his decision. 'Tied like a criminal, with real chains,' he writes.

Back in Prague, Kafka's letters to Felice become one long, endless complaint: 'I don't want to say they were good days or couldn't have been much better . . . The nastiest and indeed vilest thing is that we were never alone, except in the street, and I never had the satisfaction of a kiss from you. You could have given me one, but you didn't.'

On 21 April 1914, Franz Kafka's engagement to Felice Bauer is announced in the *Berliner Tageblatt*. An engagement party is to be held at Felice Bauer's house on 1 June. Three months later, the character 'Jozef K.' first occurs in one of Kafka's fictional diary entries. By then, the world is on fire.

At noon on Saturday 1 August 1914, the German ultimatum ordering Russia to demobilize within twelve hours and retreat from the Austrian frontier expires without a Russian reply. Within the hour a telegram goes out to the German ambassador in Saint Petersburg instructing him to declare war by five o'clock that afternoon. The tall, bald, 66-year-old warlord General von Moltke – the Chief of the General Staff who when not on duty paints, plays the piano and has begun a German translation of Maurice Maeterlinck's *Pelléas et Mélisande* – sighs: 'War, the sooner the better.'

The hour of the ultimatum passes. The stock market plunges in panic. Cars are racing down Unter den Linden with officers standing upright, waving white handkerchiefs and shouting: 'Mobilization!' Troops are already assembling at the French border. Within the hour, the first hostile act will enter the history books: the seizure of a railway junction in Luxemburg. General von Moltke writes in his diary that Europe is entering the struggle that will decide the course of history for the next 100 years.

As he does every night at exactly the same hour, the German Kaiser goes to bed at 11 p.m. sharp. For the occasion he is dressed in a military overcoat over his nightshirt. In Belgium King Albert gives orders for the blowing up of the River Meuse bridges at Liège as well as the railway tunnels and bridges at the Luxemburg frontier. In the Bois de Boulogne in Paris, the manager orchestrating a tea dance party steps forward and silences the band. He announces: 'Germany has declared war. Mobilization begins at midnight. Play the "Marseillaise".' Civilians wave and cheer; they throw bouquets of flowers at reservists who march to the Gare de l'Est. Along the Mall in London and outside Buckingham Palace, the crowds are singing 'God save the King'.

August 1914 is not only the month of 'Jozef K.', the month in which Kafka starts writing *The Trial*, it is also the month in which Edgar Rice Burroughs' novel *Tarzan of the Apes* appears. The official exchange rate is 4.20 marks to the dollar. On the Odeonsplatz in Munich, Adolf Hitler greets the proclamation of war with a beaming face. He is overjoyed. On 3 August he petitions King Ludwig III of Bavaria for permission to volunteer in a Bavarian regiment. He is afraid the war might be over before he sees action. Within 24 hours, his request is granted. He is 25 years of age. War brings him a new start in life, as a dispatch runner or message carrier in the 1st Company of the 16th Bavarian Reserve Infantry Regiment, that for the most part is made up of students and artists. Hitler arrives by train, via Mannheim, Cologne and Lille, at the front in Flanders in the third week of October after three months of training. His regiment is named the List Regiment after its commander Julius List. It is Hitler's job to carry messages between his company and the officers' headquarters. Another volunteer in the same regiment is Rudolf Hess; their administrative clerk is a sergeant-major named Max Amann.

In four days of hard fighting at the First Battle of Ypres, the British halt the German drive to the Channel. Hitler's unit is decimated. From the trenches, Hitler writes a letter to his landlord in Munich in which he confesses that his regiment is reduced from 3,500 to a mere 611 men. Only 30 officers are left alive. Julius List too has died.

August in Europe has clear, luminous mornings. Early on the 4th, 70 miles east of Brussels, an advance squadron heavily armed with sabres, pistols and rifles is crossing into Belgium. They carry 12-ft steel-headed lances, and they are dressed in brand-new, brightly coloured uniforms. Hoofs clatter over cobblestones. To the local French-speaking population they hand out printed leaflets in which they express Germany's 'regret' at being 'compelled' by necessity to invade Belgium. The German commanders trust that the Belgians will not fight against the invaders. The proclamation also warns that destruction of bridges, tunnels and railroads will be regarded as hostile acts, to be punished by death. The Belgian tricolour flag is hauled down from town halls and the imperial black eagle is raised. Now the infantry and the field artillery crosses the border, rank after rank, an endless monotony of thick, field-grey army uniforms. Cyclists speed ahead to connect telephone communication lines; in field kitchens on wheels, drawn by four horses, cooks stand up stirring the cabbage soup containing boiled beef.

Each foot soldier carries 65 lb with him: one rifle, rifle bullets, a knapsack, a pair of extra boots, tools, a knife, two tins of meat, two tins of vegetables, two packages of hard biscuits, ground coffee, a small flask of whisky and a bottle-shaped canteen for water or cold tea, bandages, thread, needles, matches, some chocolate, tobacco and eventually binoculars. As they march, the troops sing 'Deutschland Deu-eutschland über alles, über . . . alles in der Welt' (Germany above all, above all in the world).

Commander-in-chief of the rapidly advancing German troops is General Erich Ludendorff, a 49-year-old professional soldier. He is a burly, robust and unfriendly man with a drooping blond moustache and a round, double chin. For his soldiers he is an enigma, a man without a shadow. On the first day of the invasion, General Ludendorff orders his troops to shoot some Belgian priests. The tiny village of Battice is burned down; through the open windows of the flame-engulfed houses, the remnants of blackened iron beds and furnishings can be seen. Cows with unmilked udders bellow desperately in the meadows. Forlorn in the market square stands the skeleton of a roofless, spireless church.

Surprisingly, the Belgian artillery opens fire; a cannonade of field artillery, rapidly followed by an infantry assault. The German troops do not expect to be shot at; they are gloomy and nervous. Already the dead are piling up in ridges a yard high, forming an awful barricade of human flesh. Undaunted, the Belgian soldiers fire right through the wall of flesh.

A Zeppelin is sent in from nearby Cologne to bomb

the city of Liège. Field howitzers are firing right and left into the houses. With a screaming whistle, shells are falling on Liège, exploding with a deafening crash, smashing through concrete walls. A piece of artillery so colossal that it has to be pulled by 36 horses is aimed at the forts in the western part of the city. Its frightful explosion shakes the earth like an earthquake. All the windows in Liège are shattered.

The German artillery tears terrible gaps in the Belgian and French lines. Horse-drawn carts bring back the wounded: pale, bloodied, with limbs blown off. Among the first casualties is a 24-year-old lieutenant named Charles de Gaulle. The battlefield is strewn with corpses. Coal heaps around the city of Charleroi used to be black; now they are decked in blood. In the heat of a lovely summer day, 10,000 German cavalry men cross the River Meuse at Huy. In Flanders' fields, British soldiers move upwards toward their designated positions. The Belgian king at army headquarters in Louvain intends to remove the seat of government from Brussels to Antwerp. Civilians on the run block the roads everywhere. Telephone and telegraph lines are cut. In the black, tangled wires high above in the clear blue sky hang dead soldiers, blown off their feet by the explosions. In the town of Aerschot, 150 civilians are taken hostage at random and shot under the onion-like dome of the local church. Their houses are burnt down. At Dinant on the River Meuse, over 600 hostages are rounded up and massacred. Colourful posters are plastered on every house, warning the local population that anyone approaching within 200 m of an aeroplane will be shot.

On 20 August the German cavalry, with black and white pennants fluttering from their lances like knights riding out of the Middle Ages, occupy the Belgian capital of Brussels. Their black leather boots are shining; their bayonets glint in the afternoon sun. Monocled officers smoke cigarettes which they carry with them in silk-lined silver boxes. The imperial flag is raised on the town hall in Brussels, in the most beautiful Renaissance and Baroque market square in Europe. All clocks are altered to German time. An indemnity of 500 million francs is imposed on the Belgian government, payable within 10 days.

The next morning, a French cavalry patrol is mowed down by machine-gun fire in the Ardennes. In the thick fog rising from the ground, the battlefield is an unbelievable spectacle. Thousands of dead soldiers have died still standing up, rifles in hand, supported by the dead bodies of their comrades lying in rows on top of each other; dead officers wear white gloves. All over the woods, the wounded are howling and wailing. Every day, soldiers go mad.

The quick capture of the fortress of Liège and the rapid invasion of Belgium is due primarily to the work, as liaison officer, of General Ludendorff, and to his heroism in personally leading the troops infiltrating the prison fortifications of Liège. His exploits bring him to the attention of the highest military command. General Ludendorff is appointed Chief of Staff to General Paul von Hindenburg, who has been called from retirement. In the organization of the German army, a Chief of Staff often has greater influence than his commanding officer. General Ludendorff takes full advantage of this opportunity. He shows tremendous energy, and a mastery of detail in carrying out operational plans. Erich Ludendorff is awarded the blue, white and gold cross of the *Pour le Mérite*, Germany's highest military medal, but he brusquely declines the emperor's suggestion to raise him to the aristocracy.

Rudolf Hess is among the first to volunteer. Hess was born in Alexandria, Egypt, the son of a German textile importer. He attended schools in Alexandria, Bad Godesberg, Neuchâtel and Hamburg. He is immediately sent to the Western Front, first to Liège in the Ardennes, then to the north of France. He serves as a shock trooper in the same regiment as Hitler. Almost daily Hess writes long and detailed letters to his fiercely nationalist mother who lives in Reicholdsgrün, in Germany. 'Liebe Mama,' he writes in one of his letters, 'war is like a summer holiday. Against the English: Hurray! In the distance we can hear the thunder of war, but we would rather listen to some promenade music on a gramophone. Every day, we get good soup and coffee or tea with a sweetener called saccharine. Sometimes we see an aeroplane coming over. Suddenly a flash of fire on the left, then on the right. Burning villages. It is so beautiful. War!'

'I am on duty in the trenches. An officer comes by: "No news from the enemy." When it gets cold at night, we fire a few shots so that we can warm our hands on the hot rifle butts. We've got straw bags to sleep in. For lunch there is bread, sausage, some chocolate and tea. Afterwards mail and newspapers, and a cigar. Stuttering machine-guns. We don't care. A French officer shouts from his trench and asks for a German newspaper. We tell him to come over and collect it. He insists on paying 5 francs. A little later, he brings us a copy of *Le Matin*, the famous Paris morning paper. Then hostilities resume. A few artillery shots.'

'Between May and September, we conquered a hundred metres on the French. Eighty thousand Frenchmen killed, against sixty thousand Germans. From where I am sitting now, I can see dead bodies piled high up. Last night, I fell asleep next to half a Frenchman. Thank you for the butter and the tinned asparagus. I am convinced we will win this war. We're playing ball games in the trenches, and I won 10 pfennigs. Please send me a French book, preferably one by Guy de Maupassant. We exchanged bread and coffee for cigarettes with French soldiers. I am rewarded the Iron Cross. I can't stop wondering: Why, for God's sake?'

The following year, Rudolf Hess is seriously injured in the lung.

Moeller van den Bruck and his Baltic wife Lucy – they live as brother and sister – are travelling in the Scandinavian countries at the start of hostilities. To cure his alcoholic hallucinations and ever more frequent nervous breakdowns, he has entered the clinic in Denmark of Dr Daniel Jacobsen who has a reputation for treating artists, acquired after he treated Munch in the summer of 1908. Immediately Moeller van den Bruck returns to Berlin, against the advice of Dr Jacobsen who tells him that the strain of war will be too much for his fragile nervous system. But Moeller van den Bruck insists on serving his country and wearing a uniform, and he enlists as a war volunteer. 'Peace is boring,' he writes. He hastily finishes the book he has been working on, entitled *The Prussian Style*, and undergoes military training in the army barracks in Küstrin in order to become an infantry soldier second class.

Max Beckmann and his family are on vacation near

Danzig when war begins. Beckmann enlists in the army field hospital corps. Before he leaves Berlin, he vows to his wife Minna: 'I won't shoot at Frenchmen, I owe too much to Cézanne. And at Russians either, Dostoyevsky is my spiritual friend.' He is sent to the battlefields of Flanders.

As soon as his military training is finished, Moeller van den Bruck is dispatched to the Eastern Front, where he immediately collapses. He is given opium to relieve his distress and mental pain. The experience reminds him of his Thomas de Quincey translation. De Quincey mentions in his *Confessions of an English Opium-Eater* that in ancient days Homer was reputed to have known the virtues of opium as an anodyne.

There is a story which says that the Kaiser, who goes to bed wearing a military coat over his nightshirt, grew up with a crippled arm, deformed during his violent birth. The cervical nerve plexus stretching from the neck along the whole length of the left arm had been injured, while the hearing apparatus of his left ear, the so-called 'labyrinth', was badly damaged, leading to deafness and impairing his balancing mechanism. Because of insanity on both sides of his family, his nervous system was affected. At least three direct ancestors were lunatics: his great-great-grandmother, the tragic George III, and the mad Tsar Paul I of Russia, who was released from his raging lunacy by assassination.

When the future Kaiser was four years old, a German doctor offered a brutal contraption designed to force his tilted head into a more natural position. It consisted of a strong girdle worn round the middle of the body to which was fixed a steel rod reaching along the spine up to the neck with a metal collar in front which gripped the chin and held the head straight and erect. His mother Victoria, formerly Princess Royal of England and the eldest child of the reigning queen, wrote in 1870 to her mother Queen Victoria: 'Your grandson is incapable of running fast because he has no sense of balance; he cannot ride, climb, or use a knife at meals.'

In 1877, the 18-year-old prince entered the 1st Regiment of the Guards as a lieutenant and was taught the so-called 'Potsdam accent', a loud, grating, barking, rattling tone of voice, high-pitched and nasal, that cultivated several characteristics of Berlin argot and showed its upper-class quality by its maltreatment of certain vowels and consonants.

In 1880, the young prince's mother again wrote to Queen Victoria complaining about her son, the queen's grandchild: '. . . He cares nothing for sight-seeing, is absolutely not interested in works of art, does not admire beautiful scenery and never even glances at a guide book or anything that would instruct him on the places he visits.' Thirty-five years later, the young prince has become Kaiser Wilhelm II, Emperor of the Second Reich and responsible to no power but God. He visits the bombarded city of Liège and erects his headquarters in the resort town of Spa, world famous for its mineral waters.

Even in summer, the nights can be damp and cold in Flanders. The troops march in silence. When the day emerges from the morning mists, shells start exploding. Metal pellets are flying around and ripping up the wet polder ground. The troops are singing, silently at first, then at the top of their voices. Adolf Hitler is proud of his uniform. He can spend hours polishing his boots.

Occasionally he makes ink drawings and watercolour sketches of the war devastation. To Josef Popp in Munich he sends letters full of absorbing details that dwell upon deaths, corpses all around him, gun and artillery fire, dirt and dust, decaying horses. There is no fear in the letters, only excited enjoyment.

Often Hitler does the washing for his superior officers. He receives no parcels, no mail. He is a reliable, obedient and brave soldier. As a dispatch runner, he is unusually adept at running and then flinging himself to the ground and seeking shelter when the firing becomes intense. He makes careful use of maps to plot his routes. The history book of the List Regiment produces a photograph in which Hitler is seen rushing down a village street in fighting uniform, with spiked helmet and a rifle flung over his shoulder. The book also mentions that, in the thick of the fighting, Hitler covers his commander with his body. In a preface, the editor says: 'The picture of the List Regiment would not be complete without reference of the historic part that for four years Adolf Hitler served in its rank as a war volunteer on the Western Front.'

In photographs of Adolf Hitler and his wartime comrades, he stands or sits alone in a corner, aloof, with a fixed stare. He reads Schopenhauer in the trenches. The question of promoting him to the rank of officer occasionally arises, but it is decided in the negative since no leadership qualities are discovered in him. Hitler himself does not want to be proposed for promotion. He feels at home in war's no man's land.

The front line is drawn along the road from Geluwe to Beselaere; headquarters are located in the nearby villages of Wervicq and Comines, 7 kilometres to the south, a one-hour bicycle ride. Wervicq is a small farming community: a church tower, some farms and cattle barns, and a few hundred souls. A number of times a day, Corporal Hitler cycles up and down between the front line and army headquarters, delivering danger zone reports to HQ and bringing strategy scenarios to the commanding officers in the trenches.

'*Gefreiter* Hitler!' shouts the captain.

'*Zum Befehl!* answers the corporal.

Hitler tucks the march order in the *sacoche* of his bicycle and speeds off to the front, followed on his heels by Foxl, his white fox puppy. In case he loses his way, he's got a small German–French dictionary with him, in which he has inserted some rare dried herbs.

Every night at dawn, a death train is coming back from the front, mutilated corpses piled high up. Early the next morning, that same train brings newly arrived recruits to the front.

Corporal Adolf Hitler is not the only 'artist' in the trenches of Flanders. Max Beckmann has volunteered for ambulance service, and is sent to the Geluwe–Beselaere front line as well, and to Wervicq HQ, where he arrives under heavy fire. Before leaving for the front, Beckmann has agreed to submit his letters for publication in the Berlin *Kunst und Künstler* (Art and Artists) art magazine. Max Beckmann describes what Hitler must have seen: 'A wonderful, sunny, but very windy day. The Flemish landscape is flat as a board, horribly cultivated, and with nothing but long, endless straight roads. While I eat an orange, I can peacefully observe the most exquisite shooting at planes. The air is sharp as glass, clean and cold. To my left: harsh, hard shots of infantry rifles; to my right, isolated cannon shots and above all the clear sky and the sun. I constantly hear the music of this gargantuan murder. Everywhere the songs of troops, the howl of guns. I read a little in Nietzsche's *Zarathustra*.'

In his next letter: 'Incredible. The gates of eternity bursting open. The grand noise of battle. I wish I could paint that sound.' Max Beckmann keeps a diary in which he writes about his passions and turns to reflections on life, death and art. On 20 April 1915: 'Soldiers covered head to foot in clay. The music of war, the thunder of the artillery, is extremely close. From a slight elevation we look down onto the broad Flemish landscape flanked with poplars. The dark night sky marked by rockets and flares. Rats big as cats carry out the practical task of burying the corpses that lie in front of the trenches. And everywhere, the howling of the guns. Along the entire horizon nothing but horrifying grenade and shrapnel explosions. In the hospital, many of the wounded are stretched out. A young man dying, a huge bandage around his head, dark with blood. Somewhere near the left eye, you can look right through his face, as if it were a broken porcelain pitcher. He's lying in a sort of wooden box just like the typhus-infected patients.' On 26 April 1915: 'The young man has died this afternoon. The heavy guns are silent today. A large number of dead and wounded during the horrible tumult last night. This afternoon, I read Kleist's *Amphitryon* with much pleasure. Wonderful spring weather. Yesterday and last night there was a cannonade such as I never heard before. The walls trembled as if in an earthquake. The English must have been terribly angry.' On 28 April 1915: 'The front for the first time. Unforgettable and strange. All those holes and sharp trenches. Those ghostly sand tunnels. That fatal hissing of the rifle bullets and the roar of the big guns. The noise is absolutely hellish. The air is filled with the shrill whistling of shrapnel and the dark droning of the heavy guns. When the big guns tear the earth apart, the earth squeaks like a pig that is being slaughtered. Dead soldiers are carried past us. I sketched the black face of a Frenchman who stuck out partially from his grave. White crosses with their melancholy, empty helmets decorate the edges of the road.'

A few days later: 'Half-naked, blood-covered men are having white bandages applied. The punishment of Christ. The grenades from the heavy English guns begin to land even closer to us. Entire fields of house skeletons and wide, desolate plains thick with crosses, helmets, and churned up graves.'

Hitler has found a new meaning to his life. In a letter to a Munich acquaintance he writes that he participates in frontal attacks 'against an international world of enemies'. He becomes friendly with two fellow soldiers, the painter Ernst Schmidt and a Jew who answers to the name of Bachmann. He tells them that he wants to take up his profession as an architect after the war and become a political speaker. He also strikes up a friendship with a doctor from Munich, Lieutenant Fritz Braun, who is assigned to the Comines military field hospital. Lieutenant Braun is the father of a three-year-old daughter, Eva.

In four years, Hitler takes part in 47 battles. He receives the Iron Cross (Second Class) and the Iron Cross (First Class) for war bravery, but is never promoted beyond the rank of lance-corporal. On 7 October 1916, in the Battle of the Somme, he is hit in the left upper leg by a piece of shrapnel and is sent to a hospital near

Berlin to recover. In Berlin, he sees hunger and hypocrisy, war racketeering and resignation. He sends a postcard to Schmidt: 'Now I'll study the museums.' His wound is superficial; Hitler is discharged after two months and sent to Munich. After two days in Munich, he writes to his commanding officer asking to be reinstated in his regiment, because he cannot tolerate Munich when he knows that his comrades are dying at the front. According to his military passport, Hitler receives the Wounded Badge.

In March 1917 Hitler returns to the front. His comrades become frustrated with his neurotic behaviour. He harangues them about political matters and already talks about 'the next war'. They say that he doses himself with the morphine of his own words. He also compares himself with Napoleon.

After having suffered nervous and physical exhaustion, Max Beckmann is given medical leave. A Belgian doctor arranges for his transfer to Germany. Shortly before he leaves the battlefield, Beckmann writes in his diary: 'Some wounded who have been poisoned by gas roll around with uncontrolled convulsions and wheeze heavily. It is necessary to use mouth clamps to hold their mouths open.'

On the night of 13/14 October 1918, Hitler is caught in a heavy British chloride gas attack during the Third Battle of Ypres. His eyes turn into glowing coals and everything turns dark around him. He is transported from Flanders and dispatched to the military hospital for wounded soldiers at Pasewalk, north-east of Berlin, where he slowly recovers from temporary blindness.

Apart from the short and unhappy stint at the Eastern Front, Moeller van den Bruck spends the war years in the Press and News Bureau of the Political Department of the army's District Command, an information service established at the instigation of General Erich Ludendorff. Grandly called Central Agency for the Publicity and Information Service at Home and Abroad, its task is to censor all of the 1,850 daily newspapers in the German Reich while keeping the wartime propaganda machinery going. Moeller van den Bruck is in charge of improving and styling propaganda releases. He runs the war library and is jointly in charge of the Picture and Film Office, a government-financed enterprise that supervises film distribution at the front and monitors the German film companies. Also enlisted in the ranks of the Central Agency are the novelists Waldemar Bonsels, Herbert Eulenberg, Hans Grimm, Friedrich Gundolf and Börries von Münchhausen, to name but a few.

All through the war, Moeller van den Bruck publishes articles on politics, architecture, world war and race theories, Russia, Finland, Dostoyevsky, the French philosopher and writer Henri Bergson, and his hate for 'the West' and especially France. The war has crippled him, mentally and physically. As always, he seeks release in alcohol, but instead of calm he finds only further anxieties and worsening hallucinations.

Despite his suffering, Moeller van den Bruck has been able to bring to an end the writing and editing of a 755-page book, *The Italian Beauty*. Piper-Verlag in Munich agrees to publish *The Italian Beauty* with no less than 118 lavish illustrations. The book is dedicated to Theodor Däubler. *The Italian Beauty* is a dull, overlong, complex and monotonous essay on art and art history on the Italian peninsula from its origins to the Renaissance. 'Italian beauty is born in Tuscany,' writes Moeller van den Bruck, 'and the finest example of this beauty is the work of the Florentine painter Piero della Francesca.' According to the author, the Renaissance marks the beginning of decadence. 'Raphael and Michelangelo are decadent modernists.'

But no one is interested in the particular beauty of Tuscan art and architecture while war is raging and bread rations in Berlin have fallen from 2 kilos per week (two loaves of bread) to just 1 kilo, 1½ kilos of potatoes or turnips and half an egg. Church bells, organ pipes, the tin lids from beer tankards, cutlery and even pots and kitchen pans are sequestered and melted down to serve the armaments industry.

Owner of Piper-Verlag in Munich is Reinhard Piper. Although his own artistic tastes are rather conservative, he has published some of the key documents of the 'new German art', including Kandinsky's ground-breaking *Concerning the Spiritual in Art*. Halfway through publishing Moeller van den Bruck's monumental Dostoyevsky translation, Reinhard Piper asks Max Beckmann to illustrate some more episodes. Beckmann subsequently produces one illustration to *The Idiot*, the first of Dostoyevsky's novels written abroad after he left Russia to escape from his creditors, who threatened to have him imprisoned for debt. Beckmann feels a certain affinity with the novel since Dostoyevsky began working on the first draft when he lived for a short period in Berlin in the autumn of 1867.

Like most publishers, Reinhard Piper routinely publishes occasional volumes celebrating his company's anniversary. These volumes are the so-called 'almanacs'. Both Moeller van den Bruck and Max Beckmann contribute to the annual Piper almanacs directing the reader's attention to their specifically German spiritual and cultural heritage.

During the war years, the art market is much better for prints than for paintings. Reinhard Piper manages the printing and distribution of several of Max Beckmann's etchings and lithographs of war scenes, drawn while he was on duty in the trenches; he routinely mails Beckmann copies of his book publications.

The Italian Beauty could not have been published at a worse moment. Undaunted by the total lack of recognition and commercial success, Moeller van den Bruck sets out to write and publish a political pamphlet, *The German War*, in which he develops his theory that the key to the ongoing conflict and thus to world disaster is the age-old dissimilarity between the 'old countries' – Britain and France – and the 'young peoples' of Germany, Russia and perhaps America. In this pamphlet, Moeller van den Bruck insists that Germany is not a Western country. 'The West is decadent, and Germany is not,' he writes. 'Decadence is alien to the German spirit.' It is his world view that the English are 'uncultured and puritanical, devoted to a materialist class-system' while Russians on the contrary are 'religious, introvert and lethargic and mystic'. Austrians he describes as 'sleepy' and 'feminine'; Italians are 'spiritually strong'. The Germans are 'born idealists'.

His writing career is overshadowed by his growing health problems. He can only write in a veritable trance, in a state of self-induced intoxication. Pain, physical as well as psychological, dominates his life. He is convinced that everyone, everywhere, is talking about him. Munch has told him once that in his hallucinations caused by delirium tremens he imagined that newspaper reports about the hunting of wild quail referred to him. Moeller van den Bruck knows what the feeling is like. In a book on nerve diseases he reads that as long as the will to work is not weakened, there is hope of recovery. He turns his back to the artistic bohemian life he was once an integral part of and chooses to become a brooding cultural pessimist in the German tradition of Nietzsche and Schopenhauer. To his friends of former years, he becomes an enigma. The poet Franz Evers sends him a short letter: 'Twice I came to see you, and twice you shut the door in my face. What's wrong with you?'

As she has done before, his ex-wife Hedda Maase comes to his rescue. Together they start translating the collected short stories of Guy de Maupassant whose psychological realism was influenced by Gustave Flaubert, the early nineteenth-century French novelist. In his many short stories and his novels, of which the best known is *Bel-Ami*, Guy de Maupassant depicts unhappy characters who are victims of their own selfishness and sensuality. Sombre and awkward moods are therefore often described as 'Maupassant moods'. The Reclam-Bookclub in Leipzig who publishes Pascal's *Thoughts* as well as Schopenhauer and Spinoza brings out the entire edition in eight volumes under the title *Guy de Maupassant: Ausgewählte Novellen* (Selected Stories).

With Guy de Maupassant out of the way and some money in the bank, Moeller van den Bruck and Hedda (she still signs herself as Hedda Moeller-Bruck) concentrate on the German translation of *Moll Flanders* by Daniel Defoe, thought by many to be the first true novelist in the English language. *Moll Flanders*, Defoe's first novel, was written in 1683 and appeared in 1722. Its full title, *The fortunes and misfortunes of the famous*

Moll Flanders, highlights the scandalous and amoral life of Moll, a woman born and bred in the slums of seventeenth-century London. Abandoned at six months old, Moll has no option but to use her humour and good looks to make her way in the world. She embarks on a career of incest, bigamy and crime. *Glück und Unglück der berühmten Moll Flanders*, as the German translation is titled, is published at war's end by a book company called Books for Elegant Times.

Moeller van den Bruck comes out of the war an old-fashioned moralist, and a physical wreck. His bones are aching, he suffers headaches and weight loss. He often feels weak and unfocused, and has to cope with laryngitis and loss of voice. The prolific author who dashed out whole volumes in weeks has turned into a slow, calculating writer. It takes him months to get an essay right. His handwritten corrections are of an almost pedantic accuracy. He blames the deprivation of war for his worrying physical and mental condition. Sometimes he is silent for weeks on end, in a state of malaise, but he nevertheless keeps working.

Early in 1919 Piper-Verlag in Munich publishes his last title on art and architecture, *The Prussian Style*, at a price of 5 marks for the popular edition and 7.5 marks for a deluxe edition. *The Prussian Style* is a hymn in praise of monumental architecture. 'The power of the Prussian style lies in its discipline,' writes Moeller van den Bruck, himself the son of an architect. Undaunted by the neglect and the ridicule for his own literary efforts, he writes a public request to the American President Wilson, entitled *The Rights of the Young Nations*, in which he asks for mercy and clemency for Germany and German people. The appeal has the approval of the German Foreign Office. Moeller van den Bruck vows to occupy his last years exclusively with politics. He is only 43 years of age. To release him from the demons tormenting him, his friends advise him to drink milk instead of alcohol.

The German army has been beaten in the field, it is in retreat, but it has not been routed or destroyed. The victorious British and French armies are near exhaustion. They want to end the war quickly if at all possible. They do not desire the destruction of Germany: they are fighting to prove to the Germans that aggressive war cannot succeed. Even before the armistice is signed, Germany becomes a republic. The Habsburg Monarchy and the Ottoman Empire vanish, but the German Reich remains in existence. Germany is still by far the greatest power on the continent of Europe, the greatest in population also: 65 million against 40 million in France.

* * *

'HOSTILITIES WILL CEASE AT 1100 HOURS TODAY, 11 NOVEMBER.'

The war is lost. The armistice ending the unfaithful war is signed. No gunfire anymore. Many feel at a loss. Almost 3 million German soldiers are dead, over 4 million are disabled because of war wounds, and have to be supported at public expense. Berlin is littered with unemployed, drugged war veterans who have left behind homes, families and jobs. They are high on opium and morphine, sold in the streets of Berlin to relieve the persistent pain in their shot-off limbs. A blockade imposed by the Allies cuts the German Empire off from most of its overseas markets and plunges the country into deprivation. There is a casualty list in Berlin of 700,000 children, old people and women. The country is plunged into political and economic chaos. Germany is sitting on a gigantic mountain of debt, and has no access to raw materials. The bottom has fallen out of the world. A demand grows that the Kaiser should abdicate. A general strike breaks out in Berlin. Demobilized soldiers cannot find jobs; with nothing else to do, they become revolutionaries as a pastime.

'The armistice is signed, I will lead my troops home,' the chain-smoking Kaiser says.

'The armed forces will return home in peace and order under the command of their generals, but not under the leadership of Your Majesty,' his commanders reply.

The Kaiser's eyes light up in anger. He stretches himself to his full height. 'Has not every soldier sworn me an oath of allegiance?'

'In these hard times, an oath of allegiance is just a fiction,' a general says.

The Kaiser's face freezes. He abducts and flees to Holland, taking with him 60 trainloads of blankets, bedlinen and household goods.

Disguised in false whiskers and blue spectacles, General Ludendorff flees to Sweden from where he writes to his wife: 'If I ever come to power again, there will be no pardon. With an easy conscience, I will hang the instigators of our defeat and watch them dangle.'

Every kiosk and street corner in Berlin is posted with placards with the official announcement to Berliners that the Kaiser has abdicated and fled the country. Karl Liebknecht and Rosa Luxemburg, the two most efficient agitators in Germany who have spent most of the war years in prison, push for a Soviet republic. Revolution is in the air. The war which has brought death to so many millions, has it been in vain? The filth, the lice, the mud, the stench of the trenches? Three weeks after the Allies accept the terms of the armistice, Kaiser Wilhelm II mails his official abdication from his luxurious hideout in Amerongen, in Holland.

Saturday, 9 November 1918. It has started to rain before dawn, but by morning the rain has turned to drizzle. Shopkeepers pull up their iron shutters, but they haven't got anything to sell.

The *Norddeutsche Allgemeine Zeitung* (North German General Paper) carries the headline 'KAISER WILHELM II RENOUNCES THRONE'. Friedrich 'Fritz' Ebert, an artisan, trade unionist and a journalist, is appointed provisional president. He hastily forms a 'provisional workers' and soldiers' council' which issues the following declaration:

> Workers! Soldiers! Comrades! Brothers!
> People in Germany have taken the power in their own hands. Germany will be a republic – a socialist republic of workers and soldiers!

The next day, the *Norddeutsche Allgemeine Zeitung* prints the proclamation in its morning edition; by then, the name of the newspaper has changed to *Die Internationale*.

* * *

In the military hospital at Pasewalk, north-east of Berlin, Lance-Corporal Adolf Hitler is recovering from the temporary blindness suffered in a British gas attack near Ypres, on the hill south of Wervicq.

Gas in war has a powerful emotional connotation. You cannot see it, you cannot touch it, you cannot hear it, and by the time you can smell it, it is already on you, seeking out the most sensitive and precious organs of the body: the eyes and the throat. The first exposure to gas proves the final factor in upsetting a nervous system already breaking down as the result of trench exhaustion and exposure to bombardment, producing an anxiety state similar to shell-shock. Next comes the irritant reflexes such as coughing or photophobia – a condition in which a person shrinks from letting bright light fall upon the eye – or vomiting, resulting in the fear of dumbness or blindness. The acute spasm of the eyelids that characterizes the early stages of the eye lesion is treated by protecting the eye from the light. Eye shields of cotton-wool bandages are applied. It is not an uncommon thing to see a soldier, gassed months previously, groping about with eyes half closed and heavily shielded from the light, when all the actual manifestations of the eye lesion have totally disappeared.

Hitler flings himself on a bed and digs his burning head into his blankets and pillow. 'Has it all been in vain?' he cries. Hatred grows in him, and he resolves that he will enter politics if he recovers his sight.

The army has been his home for four years. He was happy to be a soldier. Again, he faces the future alone. Where to go and what to do? But how wonderful it is to recover from a long illness and see the world in a new light. After his discharge from hospital, Hitler visits Berlin and then he returns to Munich. He has no other place to go to. His adopted city is barely to be recognized. The Wittelsbach king has abdicated. A popular Jewish writer named Kurt Eisner marches through the streets at the head of a few hundred men and proclaims the republic. Not a single shot is fired. Three months later, Eisner is assassinated. A Soviet-Bavarian Republic is set up. It is short-lived.

General Ludendorff returns to Germany and settles in Munich with a host of disgruntled, discharged former army officers. Munich becomes a magnet for all those forces in Germany which are determined to overthrow the new republic – any new republic. Financed by his second wife who is a specialist in mental diseases, Ludendorff begins to devote himself to right-wing nationalist causes.

Hitler spends the winter doing guard duty and sorting out military clothing at a prisoner of war camp near the Austrian border. He is prone to overdramatization. Fear and doubts obstruct his thinking and acting. He becomes indecisive and frequently ends up doing nothing at all. The slightest difficulty can make him scream with rage or burst into tears. He has no close friends, no shoulder to cry on.

The 29-year-old Adolf Hitler, an obscure 'foreigner' with an Austrian accent who is not even allowed to vote, gets himself a job in the Press and News Bureau of the Political Department of the army's District Command. He becomes an educational officer, a *Bildungsoffizier*, whose main task it is to combat dangerous ideas such as pacifism, socialism or democracy. More accurately, he can be called a confidential agent or undercover agent in a department of the army which is keeping an eye on the numerous political splinter groups in Bavaria. Hitler looks like any ordinary young man. His dark hair falls across his forehead. One day, he receives orders from the army's Political Department to infiltrate a tiny political group in Munich which calls itself the German Workers' Party. Their formula is unused: a blend of nationalism with socialism. Hitler attends a party meeting in a dark and lifeless back room of the Sterneckerbräu beer cellar – 'more of a funeral vault than an office' – in the district of Schwabing, the artists' quarter of Munich in the north-eastern area of the city. He listens to a lecture by Gottfried Feder, a construction engineer. Feder is obsessed with the idea that 'speculative' capital is the root of much of Germany's economic trouble. Hitler is not impressed. Only 25 party members have shown up for the dull session.

Chairman of the German Workers' Party is Karl Harrer, a newspaper sports reporter, but its driving force is Anton Drexler, a locksmith by trade who is employed in the Munich railroad shops. Harrer and Drexler are the spiritual fathers of the party, together with a locomotive engineer named Michael Lotter. The party's domineering personality is Erich Röhm, a stocky, bull-necked and scar-faced professional soldier. The upper part of his nose was shot away in 1914. He is possessed with a burning hatred for the architects of Germany's defeat. 'Since I am an immature and wicked man,' he says with candid self-observation, 'war and unrest appeal to me more than good bourgeois order.' Röhm has a weakness for young males. The quintet of original party members is made up by Dietrich Eckart, a poet, dramatist, and war veteran. For Eckart, battle is synonymous with divine judgement, while artillery fire sounds to him like angels' trumpets. He has mingled with Moeller van den Bruck and his circle of bohemian friends in the 'Schwarzen Ferkel' and written a number of unproduced plays. Dietrich Eckart is a drunk who has taken to morphine. Twice in Berlin he has been confined to a mental institution where he has been able to stage his plays using the inmates as actors. He says he knows exactly what the movement needs to flourish. 'What we need is a leader who can stand the sound of a machine-gun,' he lectures. 'A common workman with no brains but who knows how to talk. And who is a bachelor so that we'll get the women voting for him.' Dietrich Eckart is a homosexual.

A few days after his first visit to the Sterneckerbräu beer cellar, Hitler receives a postcard inviting him to a committee meeting of the German Workers' Party. At first, he has no intention to attend 'this absurd little organisation' a second time. He wants to found a party of his own, eventually. But why not, after all? It is his job to infiltrate emerging political parties. He is being paid to do it, and do it well. The meeting takes place in the back room of the Alte Rosenbad beer cellar in the Herren-Strasse. Forty-six party members are gathered in the tavern, under the dim light of a gas lamp. When he enters the room, Hitler is registered as the seventh committee member of the German Workers' Party. He is not quite 31 years of age. Hitler is dressed in civilian clothes. The party coffers hold exactly 7 marks.

In Berlin, the Spartacus Manifesto – named Spartacus as a homage to the leader of the Roman slaves who revolted against their oppressors – is published in the Communist daily *The Red Flag*.

PROLETARIANS! COMRADES!
The revolution has entered Germany. For four years, soldiers were driven to the slaughterhouse for the

sake of capitalist profit. Workmen were exploited and starved to death. Together they are revolting.

Imperialism knows only one right: the profit of capitalism. Only one language: the sword. Only one method: violence. In the name of imperialism, the best men of Europe's nations were mowed down. Humanity is bleeding from a thousand wounds. Socialism alone is in a position to heal these wounds, and to transform the plains of Europe trampled down by the apocalyptical horsemen of war into blossoming gardens.

Socialism will replace hatred with solidarity, with harmony, and with respect for every human being.

Germany is pregnant with social revolution.

ARISE FOR THE STRUGGLE! ARISE FOR ACTION!

His left foot firmly planted on a machine-gun, Karl Liebknecht delivers vitriolic speeches, begging for a dictatorship of the proletariat. The Spartacists are prepared to proclaim a Soviet republic, and they are ready for it. The founding congress of the German Communist Party takes place in Berlin. As in Russia, soldiers and workmen's councils are assuming power. Guns can be bought on the streets of Berlin for less than a dollar each. Berlin is becoming a nightmare, a carnival of rattling machine-guns. Two days before Christmas, the Spartacists break into the Chancellery and cut its telephone wires.

Reichstag deputy Philipp Scheidemann sits in the dining-room of the Reichstag building (the Reich's Parliament) with some friends. They have been served a thin, watery soup. Someone shouts: 'Liebknecht is going to announce a Communist republic!'

The Reichstag building looks like a birthday cake in Italian Renaissance style. Left of the entrance is a mural of a bearded man, on the right sits a naked woman; both are surrounded by water. The man stands as the symbol for the River Rhine, Germany's boundary with France; the woman is the River Oder, the country's frontier with Poland. In the huge entry hall, in between the Rivers Rhine and Oder, rifles are stacked in pyramids – real rifles.

'Liebknecht will speak from the balcony of the Prussian Parliament Palace!'

'So what?'

'He intends to proclaim the German Soviet Republic!'

'Never!'

Philipp Scheidemann jumps the Reichstag window. Thousands of people are waving their hats, as if they've been waiting for him. The cries of the crowds echo loudly. Then, silence.

'Workers and soldiers!' shouts Scheidemann. 'We have come through four terrible years of war. But the war is over! The murdering is history! The emperor and his friends have disappeared. Do not now replace the terror of the emperor by Bolshevist terror. No! Not in Germany! Be united. Long live the German Republic!' He quickly returns to the Reichstag dining-room to finish his watery soup.

Pamphlets are distributed throughout Berlin: 'WORKERS! CITIZENS! Our Fatherland is in danger of collapse. Save it! KILL LIEBKNECHT!' The pamphlets are signed: 'The Front Soldiers'.

The Spartacists seize several newspaper offices and public buildings as well as Berlin's police headquarters on Alexanderplatz.

'Someone must be the bloodhound,' Gustav Noske says, when he accepts his appointment as Minister of

National Defence. He is a master butcher by trade, a stocky, square-jawed man of great physical strength.

Monday 6 January 1919: 11 a.m., corner of Siegesallee (Avenue of Victory) and Viktoria-Strasse. Artisans and factory girls are waving red flags. Suddenly a tremendous uproar: 'Young Liebknecht! Liebknecht's son is here!' Bloodstained, exhausted. He has been beaten up.

Saturday 11 January 1919: Façades of the old houses tower huge in the darkness. At street corners, people can be seen taking cover. Trams are still running, without lights, throwing off electric sparks which crackle like fireworks and are reflected on the wet pavement. Faces are as if cast in bronze.

Monday 13 January 1919: 10.40 p.m., an outbreak of violent fighting, with rifle-fire and the pounding and chatter of heavy and light machine-guns. Suddenly, everything is quiet. Liebknecht has disappeared. A few days later, the master butcher strikes. Front soldiers raid an apartment in the Wilmersdorf district. Liebknecht tries to escape to the Tiergarten Zoo and is shot. Rosa Luxemburg begins to scream at the top of her voice. A soldier of the cavalry division cracks her skull.

In Paris the peace terms printed in a book of 350 pages are discussed at the Peace Conference. President Wilson of the United States, Clemenceau of France and Lloyd George of Great Britain are the dominant figures. Woodrow Wilson declares that only the Kaiser and not the German people will have to pay for the defeat. No German observers are allowed to take part in the discussions. Reparations payments are imposed as compensation to the Allies for the damage caused by German arms. The British tend to let bygones be bygones and can see the eventual recovery of Germany as an important factor in the European economy. The UK's Treasury representative J.M. Keynes points out that Germany will be unable to pay all of the vast sums demanded. He suggests that Germany should be built into a great industrial nation again, able to flood the markets in the world with exports and to create a surplus over her imports. Out of this surplus, reparations could then be paid. But France insists on an everlasting weak and defeated Germany. Keynes's suggestion is brushed aside and he resigns his official position.

The terms of the Versailles Treaty are published in Berlin on 7 May 1919. They come as a staggering blow. Angry mass meetings are organized throughout the country to demand that Germany refuse to sign it. The Treaty restores Alsace-Lorraine to France; a second parcel of territory the size of Kent goes to Belgium, and a similar parcel to Denmark. It hands over to the Poles the Polish territory which Germany had taken during the partition of Poland. The Treaty forces Germany to accept responsibility for starting the war, and demands that Germany turns over 800 war criminals, among them the former Kaiser Wilhelm II and the generals Paul von Hindenburg and Erich Ludendorff.

Article 235 of the Treaty reads as follows: 'In order to enable the Allied and Associated Powers to proceed at once with the restoration of their industrial and economic life, Germany shall pay whether in gold, commodities, ships, securities or otherwise, during 1919, 1920 and the first four months of 1921 the equivalent of 20,000,000,000 gold marks.' Whatever the outcome of further negotiations, reparations payments have to be sustained for years to come. Deliveries of coal or cattle will be accepted in lieu of cash reparations. The Treaty restricts the German army to 100,000 long-term volunteers and prohibits it from having fighting planes and tanks. The navy is forbidden to build vessels over 10,000 tons. The General Staff is outlawed.

Two days before the signing of the Treaty, the *Berliner Tageblatt* correspondent in Versailles writes in the evening edition of his newspaper: 'Under the threat of bombing and hunger, we are forced to sign a document which binds us to the impossible.' On behalf of the German delegation, Count Ulrich von Brockdorff-Rantzau delivers a speech in which he warns: 'Gentlemen, we are under no illusion as to the extent of our defeat. Our strength is broken. We know the intensity of the hatred which meets us. As the guilty party, we shall be punished. But it would cost the world dear if hatred and despair should overcome the German people.' Nineteen minutes before the Allied ultimatum runs out, provisional president Ebert communicates his decision to sign the Versailles Peace Treaty to French president Clemenceau. Four days later, the treaty of peace between Germany and the Allies is signed in the Hall of Mirrors in Versailles, in the glorious palace of Louis XIV, the Sun King of France.

At five o'clock on the afternoon of Thursday 21 August 1919, Friedrich Ebert is sworn in as Reich President. One hundred and eleven women are voted into the Reichstag. The stage is beautifully decorated with the new German colours: black, red and gold. White gladioli and chrysanthemums cover the turf floor. An organ plays and the guests in their black jackets assemble between the plants. Secretaries and shorthand writers sit on the seats of the Nationalists and the Independents which have remained empty. After the organ prelude, the new president appears on the stage in a frock-coat: a small, broad-shouldered man wearing gold-rimmed spectacles. As he is about to take the oath, the text is found to be missing. Finally, someone pushes his way through the frock-coats to the front with the missing piece of paper.

For the first time, women are given the right to vote. Article 41 of the legal code stipulates direct presidential elections every seven years, article 109 that all Germans are equal before the law. Titles of nobility may be bestowed no longer. Orders and decorations shall not be conferred by the state. Article 115: the house of every German is his sanctuary; article 118: censorship is forbidden; article 137: there is no state church; article 144: the entire school system is under the supervision of the state. The prohibition of abortion is written down in articles 218 and 219. It decrees a five-year prison sentence for aborting a foetus. The new constitution signals the death of imperial Germany and the birth of the Weimar Republic.

President Ebert speaks the words of the oath in a pleasing, clear voice. Then he makes a speech. That morning, the *Berliner Illustrierte* has published a photograph of the new Reich President in a silly bathing suit.

Moeller van den Bruck, trying to cope with life in postwar Berlin, is introduced to a nobleman and a businessman who is a direct descendant of the much admired Friedrich von Schiller who, more than any dramatist and historian before or after him, is responsible for the revival of German literature. The businessman's name is Heinrich von Gleichen. He is a wealthy steel magnate. In a tavern near the Olivaerplatz in Berlin, they meet with some like-minded friends: the poet Franz Evers, the biologist Jakob von Uexküll, art critic Paul Fechter who wrote the first art monograph on Expressionism, young law student Otto Strasser and Aelbrecht Haushofer, the son of the famous Munich university professor Karl Haushofer. They agree that Berlin lacks a conservative debating club. Heinrich von Gleichen comes up with the money to rent an office. The club is called the '*i*-club' simply because Heinrich von Gleichen lives in Potsdamer Privat-Strasse 121-*i*.

New members from all walks of political life join the club: the banker Hjalmar Schacht, Heinrich Brüning (Reich Chancellor from 1930 to 1932), Franz von Papen (Reich Chancellor in 1932) and Hong Kong-born Wichard von Moellendorf who is ministerial under-secretary for Economy in the Weimar government. The novelist Hans Grimm becomes a member of the debating club. He is an acquaintance of Moeller van den Bruck from army days in the Central Agency. Hans Grimm is working on a novel tentatively entitled *Volk ohne Raum* (People without Space) in which he intends to prove that the Germans are the cleverest, most honest, most efficient and most industrious of all people, but that they live within too narrow frontiers. The conservative debating club meets in a wine cellar in the Motz-Strasse 22. The ultra-conservative Volksdeutscher Klub (German People's Club) is located in the same building. Also in the Motz-Strasse is the Café Jaenicke near the editorial offices of Ullstein publishers. Around midnight, an errand boy is sent out to collect the early edition of the morning papers from the Ullstein printing plant. When Count Ulrich von Brockdorff-Rantzau – who signed the Versailles Treaty on behalf of the provisional German government – registers for membership, they unanimously decide to rename the *i*-club the June-Club, after the month in which the Versailles Treaty was signed.

THREE
Berlin

The old imperial Berlin has been impressive. The new revolutionary Berlin is irresistible. Girls shave the backs of their necks. Music shops sell 'Tiger Rag', the first jazz record to arrive in Germany. From Holland comes the news that the exiled Kaiser is writing his memoirs. No one is interested. Hindenburg is in Berlin to answer a committee investigating war crimes. Rumours of an imminent Ludendorff coup are spreading like wildfire. War memoirs are best-sellers. Albert Einstein works in the Kaiser Wilhelm Institute of Physics that is part of Berlin University. The painter George Grosz proclaims that the artist is a maniac, and thus a sick man. Dadaism, a new 'communist' art movement, is taking the Berlin art world by storm. Rumour goes that Dadaism was invented in an 1860 Russian novel, *What is to be done?*, by the unknown Nicholas Chernyshevsky. In an aside to the lead story, two pianos are moved into a drawing-room. A lady sits at the pianos; a half chorus also forms around each piano. Then every participant sings or plays a different song, simultaneously and very loudly. The result is called: 'art' or 'the melody of revolution'.

Berlin tastes of the future. Berlin is the metropolis of the world, the *Kosmopolis*, a truly international city. Munich is different. Berlin and Munich, they are worlds apart. The difference between Berlin and Munich is the difference between the industrial west and the agricultural east, between the Protestant north and the predominantly Catholic south; between the *Plattdeutsch* speech of a Berliner and the cosy dialect of a Bavarian who finds it much easier to understand an Austrian than a Berliner. Traditionally, Bavaria is alien from Prussia and the north. Some politicians in Munich claim that Berlin is no longer part of the real Germany. Berlin is Berlin, a dynamic city populated by a lunatic generation. Germany's 10 most important cities are Berlin with over 4 million inhabitants, Hamburg with 1 million, followed by Cologne, Munich, Leipzig, Dresden, Essen, Breslau, Frankfurt and Düsseldorf. They all fade, compared to Berlin, because of their small-town atmosphere. Berlin haughtily ignores the rest of Germany and arrogantly refers to 'that flat, all too flat country'.

Munich is as cosy as its dialect, and as provincial. People from Munich lovingly call their city 'Minka', as if Munich is their puppy. Before the war, Munich was the capital of painters in the old empire, a cultural centre superior to Berlin. Drinking coffee in the Café Luitpold, within an hour you could meet the leading painters, writers and composers of the day. Franz Marc with his blue horses and August Macke painted their exotic landscapes in eccentric colours in Munich. But both painters were killed in the war, and Munich has lost out to Berlin. When Kandinsky exhibited the first abstract painting in Munich, the painting had to be wiped dry every evening because all day long visitors spat at it. The famous novelist Thomas Mann lives in Munich. He says that prewar Munich stood for democracy against militarism; postwar Munich has become a stronghold of paramilitary organizations, torchlight processions, rallies, mass parades, demagogic speeches, ruthless attacks on political opponents and revolt against the chains of Versailles.

Of course Berlin hates the legacy of the lost war and the Versailles Treaty as much as Munich does, but Berlin is different. While in Berlin the liberal intellectual grabs the limelight, the anti-liberal conservative right is silently present everywhere. For a while they truly believed that in the aftermath of the fighting a new world had been born; that the shock of defeat would throw the whole world wide open. Their hopes were false hopes, and despair followed. The conservative right hates the new, 'artificial' Weimar Republic and despises its culture. Weimar signals decay and moral bankruptcy. The new spirit is the spirit of degeneration and cultural Bolshevism. A Berlin police officer asks: 'New culture?' And replies: 'It ought to be liquidated!' Left-wing and right-wing writers are not on speaking terms. Intellectuals of the left are Francophiles; they stand for close collaboration with Germany's neighbours, in particular with France, its traditional and historical arch-enemy. The cultural critic and literary journalist Walter Benjamin, a master of the German language, announces that he can no longer write in German and he starts writing in French, a language in which he expresses himself not without difficulty. The left idealizes everything French, the right blames France for the downfall of Germany. The right is convinced that the left is anti-patriotic; the left claims that the right is stupid and barbaric. There is no room for compromise. There is no middle ground. If they have one thing in common, it is probably that both are unhappy.

On a cold and wet winter morning late in February 1920, Bertolt Brecht arrives in Berlin. To his friend Caspar Neher, who has stayed behind in Munich, he writes: 'Everything is overflowing with dreadful lack of taste.' For three weeks, Brecht lives on pea and bean soup and all the bread you can eat at Aschinger's, a popular and inexpensive restaurant. The recipe for the soup is created by a Nobel prize-winning scientist. Then Brecht returns to Munich. The first taste of Berlin has not made him too hungry.

On 31 March 1920 Hitler is demobilized. As a farewell present, he receives a hat, an army coat, a jacket, a pair of trousers, a pair of underpants, a shirt, a pair of shoes and a total of 51 marks, described as 'survival money'.

Now that he is a registered committee member himself, Hitler takes command of the small German Workers' Party. He starts typing invitations to party meetings and distributes the invitations himself. When no one shows up, he has the invitations mimeographed: he fastens his typed text to a drum which is inked on the inside; with each revolution of the drum, the ink penetrates the stencil and a new copy is made. He inserts the notice of a party meeting in a local newspaper. One hundred and eleven people attend the meeting. Adolf Hitler makes his first public speech. He emphasizes the ideas he has absorbed in Vienna: anti-Semitism, extreme nationalism, hatred, the concept of Aryan racial supremacy, contempt for liberal democracy, and the principle of authoritarian leadership. He expresses hate of the blacks, Czechs, Poles, Russians and all other non-Aryans whom he considers fit only to be the slaves of the Germans. The audience is 'electrified' by his oratory. Donations of up to 300 marks flow in. The party is relieved of its financial worries.

Accompanied by Max Amann, his former administrative clerk in the trenches of Flanders, Hitler goes to a large store in the old part of Munich and buys office furniture. The furniture is paid for in Czech banknotes, which are legal tender in Munich. He also gets hold of a second-hand American rotary machine.

Every Monday evening, Hitler holds a party meeting. He invariably laments about the Versailles Treaty and the defeat of the Fatherland. As he did to his comrades in the trenches, he speaks of 'the next war' and compares himself to Napoleon. Blood and race are his main theme. Hitler glorifies man's brutality as essential to human accomplishment. His speeches are not spontaneous; he spends as many as eight hours on the preparation of one single sermon.

Hitler is made responsible for party propaganda. A wealthy Munich-based publisher of art posters named Putzi Hanfstäengl, whose wife is an American Harvard socialite, loans the party 1,000 dollars, a fortune in that inflation period. A Baltic adventurer named Max Erwin von Scheubner-Richter joins the party. He is an actor by profession who was a Russian agent in Constantinople during the war. He teaches Hitler some acting techniques and convinces the White Russians who have been driven out of their homelands by the Bolsheviks to contribute to the National Socialist Party. Munich is the centre of White Russian immigration, even more so than Berlin.

Hitler starts organizing the biggest meeting ever dreamt of by the small party initiated and created by a locksmith, a drunken poet, an economic crank, a ruthless war veteran and a failed artist. The meeting is to be held in the famous Hofbräuhaus. It has a seating capacity of nearly 2,000. His fellow party members think Hitler has gone crazy. Karl Harrer resigns as party chairman. For personal reasons, Michael Lotter also steps down. The main speaker at the Hofbräuhaus party rally is a certain Dr Johannes Dingfelder, a homeopathic physician who contributes articles on economy to a local Munich newspaper under the pseudonym of Germanus Agricola.

Dr Dingfelder's speech is greeted with silence. Then Hitler stages a dramatic arrival and begins to speak. His voice is capable of extraordinary shrillness and penetration. By resorting to biting sarcasm, verbal attack and preached hatred, he knows how to stimulate his audience and keep them hanging onto his words for three hours. His attack on the Versailles Treaty wins him a thunderous applause. For the first time, he reads out the 25 points of the ideological party programme that has been drawn up by Drexler, Feder and himself.

The very first point in the programme demands the union of all Germans in a Greater Germany. Jews are to be denied office and excluded from the press; they are even to be denied citizenship in Germany altogether. The second point demands the termination of the Versailles Treaty. There is screaming and shouting in the Hofbräuhaus, and violent clashes break out between party supporters and Communists and socialists. Point 16 insists on the lease at cheap rates of department stores to small traders. Point 18 demands the death penalty for traitors and profiteers. Germanic law should replace Roman law. The facilities for taking care of the elderly should be much expanded. Only people of German blood can be German citizens. Jews will be regarded as temporary guests. If nourishment to feed all the country's inhabitants grows insufficient, the temporary guests will be deported. The last point, number 25, insists on the creation of a strong central power of the state.

When Hitler asks his audience if the Germans

can defend themselves against the Jews, shouts from the audience provide the answer: 'Hang them! Kill them!' Hitler chooses a vocabulary of poison, disease, corruption, 'liquid manure', 'abscesses', 'racial maggots', and promises 'lampposts full of corpses' and 'heads rolling'. To decapitate, as Dr Freud points out, means to castrate in the mind of the psychopath. Half an hour after Hitler has delivered his speech, the thunderous applause begins to drown out the screaming and shouting.

Then Hitler speaks in the Krone Circus in Munich. Among the crowd of 6,500 is a young Rhinelander from Reydt near Cologne. His name is Paul Joseph Goebbels. That night he exclaims in his diary: 'I am reborn! Now I know which road to take!' To a friend, Hitler confides: 'It is a sublime feeling to walk through a cheering crowd. One becomes a different man.'

Hitler starts forming the party into a paramilitary organization. As an ex-soldier, he uses his influence with his demobilized comrades and persuades a number of them to join his union of disgruntled war veterans. The party expands its name to National Socialist German Workers' Party, that will remain the permanent name of the Nazi Party. Over the next six months, Hitler delivers at least 28 speeches in Munich and elsewhere. He revisits Austria, of which country he is still a citizen, and speaks in Vienna, Innsbruck, St Pölten and in his native town of Braunau. He never mentions any of his Austrian family members. Hitler compares himself to God, and God obviously does not have brothers or sisters, brothers-in-law or sisters-in-law, nephews and nieces.

About 50 party members accuse Hitler of inordinate ambition. They petition with a placard which reads:

'Adolf Hitler is power-mad. He believes himself to be the King of Munich.' Time and again, Hitler screams and shouts the same catchphrases: 'National Socialism is more than a religion. It is the recreation of mankind!' Or: 'Brutality is respected. People want something to frighten them.' Anti-Semitism he regards as a means of mobilizing the masses. The local Munich press calls 'the leader of the anti-Semite party' an extremely cunning talent as a demagogue.

A bunch of roughneck war veterans are drilled into 'strong-arm' squads under the command of Emil Maurice, an ex-convict and watchmaker. They are officially named the *Sturmabteilung* or Storm Troopers, and are outfitted in surplus uniforms from the war. Boys are dressed in brown flannel blouses. Hitler teaches them the special Nazi salute with extended arm and hand. What the party lacks is an emblem and a flag that express what his organization stands for and appeals to the masses. Hitler hits upon the symbol of a red background with a white dish in the middle in which is imprinted the hooked cross – the *Hakenkreuz* – of the black swastika, in the old imperial colours: black, red and white, 'the most brilliant harmony in existence'. Hitler says that the swastika symbolizes the struggle for victory of the Aryan man. Distributing the new insignia to his Storm Troopers, Gregor Strasser explains: 'Red signifies the social orientation of our party, white symbolizes our love for the Fatherland, and the black swastika is the wheel that will crush any foreign race which tries to pull our country under.'

Flanked by his personal bodyguards, Hitler silences a monarchist by assaulting him on a public platform. He is taken to court and serves one month of a three-month prison sentence. At evening parties, Hitler wears a cartridge belt with a loaded revolver. From its first appearance, the swastika exhibits a machine-like power and terror. Dietrich Eckart comments: 'Something has gone wrong with Adolf . . . shouting "I must enter Berlin like Christ entered the Temple!"' Max Amann becomes the first managing director of the Nazi Party.

Hitler begins working on a book in which each chapter is approached as a speech. Its original title is *A Reckoning*.

On the surface, life is fun again. 'At Home I Have a Gram a Gram a Gramophone' is a huge hit. The gramophone also popularizes the voice of Italian tenor Enrico Caruso. In Leipzig a fair is held. Innovations are wooden shoes and paper clothes that cannot be washed, which is as well since soap is in short supply. A workday in the factory begins at 6 a.m. sharp, lunch box in hand. Factory workers work nine and a half hours a day. Saturday is a day off. Six days of vacation, once a year; ideal for spring cleaning.

New service industries such as banks, insurance companies, commercial enterprises, bring a growing number of white-collar workers. They dress better than manual workers, and they live in nicer homes. The number of bank employees triples and the number of active accounts at the three big 'D' banks – Deutsche Bank, Dresdner Bank, Darmstädter Bank – grows fivefold. While the factory worker can be fired from one day to the next, white-collar employees may be dismissed only four times a year and have to be given six weeks' notice. Banks and insurance companies are advised to preserve the employees' feelings of duty and pleasure at work since it is believed that the rationalization of office operations is monotonous, kills interest and stresses the nerves. The claim is made that the workforce will be reduced to slaves of the new office machines which are outfitted with 'automatic-control mechanisms' that indicate operator errors 'by means of trouble signals or by blocking the mechanism'. The social effect of office machines troubles employees: they have no need of memory because the processes run mechanically and, even worse, someone else can quickly take their place. At the newly constructed Ford plant in Cologne, the first Ford automobile will soon roll off the assembly line. 'Fordism' promotes set work norms, higher wages, employee loyalty and a leisure ethic, as well as efficiency and elimination of labour conflict.

'Americanism' is everywhere. Commentators openly acknowledge the profit-driven 'Yankee civilization' influenced only by America. American culture captures and colonizes the German imagination: Charlie Chaplin, jazz, boxing, skyscrapers, Henry Ford, chewing gum, Chicago gangsters are the talk of the day. A swindler in Hamburg takes out an advertisement seeking engineers for work in South America. He receives 4,000 responses in one single day.

A water system is installed in Berlin. In old houses and office blocks, staircases are broken away and replaced by elevators. Peter Behrens who is chief designer for the AEG electric company incorporates geometric simplicity into pre-war buildings and captures the popular imagination with an innovative choice of materials: coloured glass, surfaces made of windows, reinforced concrete, brightly painted walls. Architect Bruno Taut proclaims: 'Today, there is no art.'

He is responsible for the Glass Pavilion in Cologne and for several Berlin workers' housing projects. He wants to erase the frontier between the applied arts and the fine arts so that it will become one thing only: architecture. Taut proposes glass as a building material and wants to build lightweight large-scale housing estates not inside the town but in the open country.

Public lavatories burst upon the local scene, as well as Burrough's calculating machines, the parlograph, Fokker and Farman civil aircraft not at all respectful of national borders, the radio, the Marconigram, Faenza sinks, His Master's Voice, Vox, psychoanalysis, graphology, pre-sized stationery, gasoline stations, concrete pylons, mass apartment blocks, the League of Nations, tennis shoes, Havana cigars, windows extending all the way down to the ground, bachelor apartments, flat roofs, metal furniture, stain remover, chocolate containing nuts, and the folding chair.

People live faster and longer. The step-by-step mechanization of the planet is not to be stopped, or so it seems. There is a counter-culture. Equipment in laboratories marked in 'amperes' – units of measure of electric current named in honour of a French scientist – is renamed 'weber', a German scientist. When Walther Rathenau is appointed Foreign Minister, a right-wing paper writes: 'Now we have it! Germany has a Jewish Foreign Minister! His appointment is an unheard-of provocation!' People in the street start chanting: 'Shoot down Walther Rathenau, that Goddamned Jewish swine!' Discipline, courage – the virtues of soldiers and heroes – have become meaningless. The Fatherland fades away. Worse still, the Fatherland House in Berlin is transformed into a popular amusement hall.

Within a few short years, Berlin has become the metropolis of conflicting contrasts. Berlin is for Germany what Paris is for France. Everything must be Berlinized. No city in the world is as restless as Berlin. Everything moves. A man walks the street playing two drums at once. He has a hook on his right ankle with a string to the kettledrum on his back. When he stamps his foot, a drumstick strikes the drum and bells attached to it cling together. In the basement in the rear of a building on Kurfürsten-Strasse lives a tailor who collects imperial memorabilia, such as family photographs of the last Kaiser with his children, grandchildren and great-grandchildren around him. When a woman is old, it is said that she still has hair from the last century on her head. The conservative right hates the new Berlin. They long for the Berlin of old. Moeller van den Bruck proclaims publicly: 'Our German Kaiser Wilhelm II wanted to turn Berlin into the most beautiful city in Europe. Look at it. Berlin is in ruins.'

Magnus Hirschfeld opens the first Institute of Sexual Science in Berlin. It is devoted to all aspects of sexuality. The institute is visited for premarital consultation and instruction as well as for legal and medical research. Uppermost on the agenda of the institute is its campaign against Article 175, the law in Germany's penal code against male homosexuality. Since 1895 Hirschfeld has been a pioneer in the struggle for the right of the 'third sex', as he calls homosexuals. The Institute publishes sex manuals providing education about modern sexual practices and techniques and serves as a consultant for Richard Oswald's semi-documentary film *Different from the others*. Hirschfeld is a practising homosexual, a Communist, and a Jew. In Berlin he can walk the street unmolested. When he is lecturing in Munich, he is twice assaulted by right-wing groups.

Berlin is the city of theatres. Bertolt Brecht's post-expressionist *Drums in the Night* opens at the Deutsches Theater. The play is set against the background of the Spartacus uprising three years previously. It is a drama of personal relationships punctuated by the sounds of gunfire. Shots echo and re-echo, accompanied by the singing of the 'Internationale'. Nothing but the starkest realism and reality. The stage directions conclude: 'His laughter is choked; he staggers; he hurls the drum at the moon, which in reality is a lantern, and drum and moon topple into the river, which has no water in it.' The conservative right sees it differently. 'Theatre today has sunk to lower depths than ever,' writes the critic Hanns Johst. Bertolt Brecht is back in Berlin and he is the talk of the town. He is 24 years of age. He is dressed in an old leather bomber jacket, like some secret commissar of a mysterious Moscow propaganda agency. But not only his attire is unconventional. 'His head is shaved like a convict of Sing Sing, and he wears a steel-rimmed pair of glasses,' recalls the journalist Willy Haas.

Even classical plays break with stage conventions. The set of Schiller's *Wilhelm Tell* is reduced to nothing but huge stairs spanning the entire stage. This allows the actors to move not only horizontally but also vertically. As the play is situated in Switzerland, maps of Switzerland and the Alps are pinned onto the stage.

In 1910, the critic Karl Scheffler called Berlin a city doomed to a perpetual state of 'becoming' but never completed, but the recently created Greater Berlin is the third largest city in the world, after New York and Los Angeles. The experimental playwrights and directors work and live in Berlin, the influential critics, the artistic directors, the most celebrated actors and actresses of the day. New theatres, cinemas, swimming-pools, racetracks, office buildings, factories, exhibition halls, luxury apartments and flats are being built.

A 21-year-old actor named Max Goldmann comes to Berlin. At the Deutsches Theater he directs plays by Strindberg, Wedekind, Oscar Wilde and Gorki. He changes his name to the less obviously Jewish name of Max Reinhardt and widens his repertoire to include Shaw and Shakespeare, Schiller and Goethe. A 3,000-seat converted circus on the Schumann-Strasse becomes the new home of the Deutsches Theater.

Life in Berlin is dazzling. A nonchalant approach to sex is considered absolutely chic, and a way of getting through the monotony of everyday life. Bare-breasted prostitutes chat with customers at the Café Nationale. Boys and girls in black leather and shiny boots are posted at street corners. New theatre shows are imported from London and New York. Gossip about the theatre is of major interest to the Berlin tabloids. The famous novelist Thomas Mann is in Berlin for discussions about a film of his *Buddenbrooks* novel that has sold over 1 million copies since it was first published. His 19-year-old daughter Erika is employed by Max Reinhardt as a small-part actress. Berliners are reading in best-selling quantities the translated works of Herman Melville, Walt Whitman, Mark Twain, Edgar Allan Poe and Dostoyevsky. Every month, a new English tearoom opens in Berlin. Emigrant Russians who have fled the revolution desert Paris for Berlin because of sharply rising prices in Paris. Life in Berlin is absurdly cheap, only a quarter of what it costs to live in Paris or London.

Among the first Russian refugees to set up home in Berlin is the pianist Vladimir Horovitz. From Cambridge comes writer Vladimir Nabokov with his family. On 28 March 1922 his father is accidentally killed in a shoot-out in the Berlin Philharmonic. Nabokov will remain in Berlin for another fourteen and a half years. Russian publishers settle in Berlin and produce books in Russian that are sent back to Russia where books are in short supply after the chaos of civil war. Gamayun is one of many new Russian publishers in Berlin. He commissions Nabokov to translate Lewis Carroll's *Alice in Wonderland* into Russian. Nabokov finds the translation easy work. In the Russian version, Alice becomes Anya. One day, Nabokov is dining in the restaurant section of the Café Leon on Nollendorfplatz. Aleksey Tolstoy is sitting at a nearby table. Nabokov ignores Tolstoy, who is pro-Soviet. 'As a White Russian,' he remarks casually, 'I do not wish to speak to a *Bolshevizan.*' Tolstoy begins to write for the daily newspaper *Nakanune* that is established with Soviet funding. As a result, he is excluded from the Union of Russian Writers and Journalists in Berlin.

The Russians refer to the Charlottenburg district as 'Charlottengrad' while the Kurfürstendamm becomes 'Kurfürsten-Prospekt'. Russian emigrants have a preference for the Lichterfelde district around the Russian teashop in the Kleistrasse. The city has its own Russian newspaper, *Rul*, backed by Ullstein and distributed throughout the world. The literary cafés frequented by Russians provide a fertile meeting ground for writers who have aligned themselves with the Soviet regime, those who are opposed to it, and those who are still undecided.

Eighty-six Russian publishing houses have been established in Berlin. Within four months, Nabokov publishes four books in Russian under his pseudonym Sirine: two translations and two verse books – *Gorny poet* (Way to Heaven) and *Grozd* (Grapes). He is very much part of the bustle of literary Berlin. While walking through the city centre, the chestnut trees in flower, Nabokov describes Berlin night life as 'the tangerine tinge of premature shop lights'. He calls himself 'a poet in his prose'. Nabokov loves a ride on the city's yellow trams.

On Kurfürsten-Prospekt a Russian cabaret opens. It prints its own trilingual journal, *Karussel/Carousal/Carrousel*, with illustrations of sets, scenes, costumes, articles and poems evoking the flavour of the Russian cabaret. Nabokov contributes under different pen names: Vladimir Sirine, Vladimir V. Nabokoff and V. Cantaboff. He is teaching tennis, boxing and languages but resolutely declines to learn German. He prefers to speak French. Nabokov reads his work in the Schubert Room in the Bulow-Strasse as part of a literary evening on the subject of Russia. The evening is organized by the Russian Nationalist Students' Union. Here he meets Véra Slonim, his future wife. 'I won't find a better wife,' he writes, 'but do I need a wife at all?' Occasionally, Nabokov renders the Russian correspondent's articles for the *Westminster Gazette* and *The Times* into acceptable English.

The new cinema flourishes. There are over 275 film companies in Berlin. Each year, 400 films are produced in Berlin alone: romances, thrillers, horror films, even German Westerns. On top of that, Hollywood floods the German film market with comedies and action pictures. The German expressionist film style typified by Robert Wiene's silent horror tale *The Cabinet of Dr Caligari* which is set in an insane asylum, Paul Wegener's *The Golem*, F.W. Murnau's *Nosferatu* and Fritz Lang's anarchic thriller *Dr Mabuse* completely alters the language of film. 'Cocaine or playing cards?' a shady character asks the undercover detective in *Dr Mabuse*. The film tells the tale of a criminal mastermind pursuing wealth and power against the background of hyperinflation. Director Fritz Lang says his film is directly influenced by the exploits of Al Capone.

Debates centre around the issue of cinema's artistic potential. How can cinema ever become an art form? As they are silent films, the essence is how to communicate without language at all. German expressionist cinema puts the emphasis on style and abstraction over the realism of Hollywood. Atmosphere, camera movement and composition take precedence over character development and action. Theatre and film actor Emil Jannings describes the impetus behind the popular crime film as a romantic longing for adventure and danger in the midst of modern reality and rationality. Expressionist film features mad scientists, inventors, robots that rebel against their creator, golems, vampires and doppelgänger.

Alfred Hitchcock, Billy Wilder and Fred Zinnemann come to Berlin to make films at the Universum Film Agency's new studios, which offer the finest technical facilities in the world.

While modern film flourishes, there is no sympathy at all for abstract painting, nor for the 12-tone atonal music of Arnold Schoenberg and Alban Berg. The new art has little appeal and no message. Modern classical music sounds anti-romantic and anti-sentimental.

Literature takes on a hard, cold, masculine tone. Expressionist painters such as Karl Schmidt-Rottluff, Ernst Ludwig Kirchner, Erich Heckel and Max Beckmann are fascinated by ugliness. Beauty is a lie, disfiguration is reality. Even the sun stinks.

There is this darker side of Berlin. Five hundred assassinations in street riots are registered over a two-year period. Violent crime accompanies massive unemployment and shortage of homes. The food scarcity is terrible. The artist George Grosz calls Berlin 'a completely negative world, with gaily coloured froth on top that many people mistake for true food'. An influenza epidemic claims the life of 1,700 people in one single day. Stefan Zweig writes that Berlin has transformed itself into the Babel of the world. Casual sex and opium are easily available. The novelist Alfred Döblin describes sexual activity in sports terms. In the bar of the noble Hotel Adlon, unemployed army officers and aristocrats fallen on hard times work as gigolos. The comic cabaret where the satires of Kurt Tucholsky draw an international audience has interludes with topless dancers. Tucholsky calls Hitler 'a house painter' who 'bestows ridiculous titles' on his followers.

Nothing is censored. Every kind of sexual taboo is challenged. The German society known for its authoritarian discipline is fast disappearing. To those who survived the horrors of war, laws and regulations appear to be irrelevant. There is a swift decline in moral standards. Writers and painters from all over the world flock to Berlin not only because of the cultural attractions of the metropolis but because of the easy availability of cocaine from South America and opium, as well as 'alcohol, nicotine, tea, coffee, morphine, marijuana, chloral hydrate, ether, soporifics'.

Gambling is widespread, prostitution common. Crime is rampant. Clever bank robbers, serial killers and successful con men monopolize headlines and capture the imagination of millions of Germans. The number of executions of criminals sentenced to the death penalty totals 28 per year. The German judicial system leaves almost 400 political murders unpunished – 354 by the right, against 22 by the left. Before the war, a kilo of cocaine cost 16 marks, and was sold in chemists' shops only. In 1921, cocaine is offered at 17,000 marks per kilo on the high street. On the black market, it is obtained under the name 'cement', 'coke' or 'cocoa'. A sausage seller has set up shop in the doorway of a gambling club in the city centre. 'Pure pork!' he guarantees. On the side, he does a booming retail trade in cocaine. Heroin is sold under the trade name 'H'.

There is a fashionable new hairstyle: sleek and brushed straight back. Liselotte de Booy is the first Miss Germany. New words such as 'sex appeal', 'cocktail', 'flirt' and 'jazz' find their way into the German language. Advertisements are the new literature for non-readers. Billboards ask the question: 'Who knows Pascal?' Pascal is a French philosopher and mathematician. The answer: 'Everyone knows Odol!' Odol is a brand of mouthwash.

A teacher in Berlin's working-class district named Adolf Koch begins conducting gymnastics classes in the nude, justifying it on the grounds that nudity makes everyone equal. He traces nudism back to its Hellenic roots. Nudism promises to reclaim the body that is lost at the assembly line in the new factories. It also awards a feeling of national and racial superiority.

Boxing is promoted as the most noble of all sports, praised for its refreshing anti-intellectualism. Hundreds of thousands are shaken by the defeat of German boxing champion Hans Breitensträter. The sports stadium replaces the art museum. Dr Carl Diem (who by 1936 is in charge of the Berlin Olympics) becomes responsible for Berlin's municipal sports programme. His 'physical culture movement' aims to promote military practice, discipline, racial superiority and national survival.

The artist Kurt Schwitters insists he is making a political statement by festooning the walls of his home with junk yard garbage. Revolution and murder are as common as prostitutes and beggars in the street. Stefan Zweig writes in his diary: 'Along the entire Kurfürstendamm hundreds of men dressed as women and women dressed as men dance under the eyes of the police.'

The mark begins to slide and drops to 75 to the dollar. That is bad, but bearable. The Weimar government simply prints some more money. By 15 November 1921, the dollar costs 258 marks. It falls to 400, then to 7,000. The printing presses of newspapers are ordered to print money in ever larger denominations. Entire fortunes of those who have invested in gold and treasures are wiped out. Berliners pay 600 marks to ride the trolley buses. A pint of milk costs 1,440 marks. Because he can't buy paint, Kurt Schwitters pastes paper money into his collages. People start exchanging goods for services: two eggs can buy you a haircut. On top of the price of a cinema ticket, you have to bring two bricks of coal to help with the heating. Money is carried to the bank in laundry baskets. At the homes of the rich, bundles of money become toys for children. The Weimar government can't understand what is happening and asks the Allies for a moratorium on reparations payments. The mark falls to 18,000 to the dollar. The government keeps printing money, working overtime. Bavaria agitates against what is called 'the Jewish Republic of Weimar'. Bitterness increases because the Weimar Republic gives German Jews equal rights, at least on paper.

Law student Otto Strasser is spending the summer holidays at the house of his parents in the rural town of Deggendorf in Bavaria. He receives a telephone call from his brother Gregor, who is a pharmacist. A second brother, Paul, has taken orders and has become a Benedictine monk. On the outbreak of war, all three volunteered. Otto was only fourteen years of age. Ever since that fateful day on 1 August 1914, one single question has been nagging him: how to translate the comradeship of the trenches into a true socialist community in civilian life?

'Come and have lunch tomorrow with General Ludendorff and Adolf Hitler,' says Gregor. He is living with his young wife in Landshut, about 60 miles from Deggendorf.

Otto Strasser takes the early train and walks from the station under a clear blue sky. A beautiful car is standing in front of the chemist's shop in the Landshut high street. General Ludendorff, who is the idol of Germany's patriotic youth because of his war record, is a strong man, with heavy features and a firm double chin. In spite of his civilian clothes, he looks every inch a general. He gazes at Otto Strasser from under his bushy eyebrows. Hitler wears a dark suit.

They sit down for lunch.

'Your brother has spoken to me about you,' Ludendorff tells Otto Strasser. 'How many years of service have you done?'

'Four and a half years,' Otto Strasser replies. 'At fourteen, I was the youngest Bavarian volunteer. I served as a second lieutenant and as a lieutenant. I was in the army from 2 August 1914 to 30 June 1919. Twice I was wounded.'

'Bravo!' Ludendorff says, and he raises his wineglass in a toast. Hitler's glass contains only water. 'Herr Hitler does not drink alcohol,' explains General Ludendorff. 'He is also a vegetarian.'

At that moment, Gregor's wife Else brings in the roast. 'Herr Hitler will not offend me by refusing my cooking,' she says calmly. Enclosed in a hostile silence, Hitler eats his meat.

After lunch, the four men retreat to a dark sitting-room with heavy oak furniture. The general, reclining in a leather armchair, smokes a cigar. Hitler keeps pacing up and down the room. Suddenly he confronts Otto Strasser.

'Herr Strasser,' he says, 'I do not understand how it is possible for a loyal ex-officer like you to have been a leader of the *reds* in Berlin and participate in the red revolution.'

'My *reds*, Herr Hitler, were not rebels, as you seem to suggest, but patriots.'

Hitler works himself into a state of excitement. 'The Weimar government must be overthrown!' he says nervously. 'I wish to inflame the people with the idea of revenge! Only total fanaticism can make us win the next war!'

'There is no question of revenge and neither of war,' Otto Strasser replies. 'Our only aim is to establish a new order in Germany.'

'Yes,' agrees Gregor.

'Playing about with ideas like yours is useless,'

Moeller van den Bruck as an Intelligence Officer, First World War. (Staatsbibliothek, Berlin)

Adolf Hitler in mid-speech.
(© *Illustrated London News*)

Heinrich Himmler.
(© *Illustrated London News*)

Revolution is in the air: the Spartacus uprising, Berlin, 1919.
(© *Bundesarchiv ONB, Vienna*)

Edvard Munch: portrait of Friedrich Nietzsche, 1906–7. Oil on canvas; Munch Museum, Oslo. (Photo: Munch Museum (Svein Andersen/Sidsel de Jong), © Munch Museum/Munch-Ellingsen Group/DACS, London, 1999)

Rosa Luxemburg walking in the Berlin Grünewald district. (© Ullstein Bilderdienst)

Max Beckmann as an ambulance volunteer on the Western Front, 1914–15. (© Bayer Staatsgemäldesammlungen/Max Beckmann Archiv, Munich)

Edvard Munch: The Brooch, 1903 lithograph, Munch Museum, Oslo.
(Photo: Munch Museum (Svein Andersen/Sidsel de Jong), © Munch
Museum/Munch-Ellingsen Group/DACS, London, 1999)

Max Beckmann posing in front of his large 1913 painting *Sinking of the 'Titanic'*. (© Bayer Staatsgemäldesammlungen/Max Beckmann Archiv, Munich)

Marlene Dietrich. (© *Illustrated London News*)

Otto Strasser. (Photo courtesy of the Wiener Library)

Book burning in Opera Square, Berlin. (Photo courtesy of the Wiener Library)

Berlin Olympics opening ceremony, 1936. (© *Illustrated London News*)

Adolf Hitler. (© *Illustrated London News*)

exclaims Hitler. 'What *I* am talking about is reality, and reality is Jewry. Marx is a Communist Jew and Foreign Minister Rathenau is a capitalist Jew. All evil comes from the Jews who pollute the world. Jews control the press. Their aim is the destruction of our nation. Jews talk of improving the lives of the workers. In reality, they enslave the working class in order to establish the international dictatorship of Jewry. What a Jew cannot achieve by persuasion, he will try to achieve by force. Their organization is flawless. Jews have their fingers in every pie. They are an ulcer leading to the downfall of nations and individuals.'

'You overestimate the Jews, Herr Hitler,' Otto Strasser says. 'Socialism has more than one face. Marx worked in collaboration with Engels, who was a good German. Marzinni who examined the religious and national implications of socialism was an Italian. Bakunin developed the nihilist side of socialism out of which Bolshevism was born, and he was Russian. You see, socialism is not at all of Jewish origin.'

'Certainly not,' agrees General Ludendorff.

Hitler changes tack. 'I wish to give the German people a touch of the whip to pull them together so that they will be capable of crushing France,' he snaps.

'I certainly do not approve of the Versailles Treaty myself,' Otto Strasser replies, 'but fighting France seems stupid to me. The day will come when France and Germany will have to unite to fight Russian Bolshevism.'

Hitler makes an impatient gesture.

His cigar smoked, General Ludendorff rises. He says goodbye and leaves, followed on his heels by Hitler.

'Well?'

'I like Ludendorff,' says Otto Strasser. 'He is certainly

not a brilliant man, but he behaves like a gentleman. As for Hitler, he is just a walking loudspeaker.'

'Perhaps,' replies Gregor Strasser. 'But Hitler has a magic quality which is difficult to resist. What fine things we could do if we could use Hitler to express our ideas and Ludendorff's energy and charisma to carry them out.'

Shortly afterwards, Gregor Strasser becomes the Nazi Party's first *Gauleiter* or chief official of a political district under Nazi control.

What is happiness? To this question, Tolstoy gives a simple answer: 'Happiness is living in and with nature.' The architect Bruno Taut concludes that city dwellers in Germany must all be unhappy, since living conditions in German cities are among the worst in Europe. Cramped and unsanitary flats usually house more than one family. Local housing codes are lax. In Berlin, the situation is especially dire. Nineteenth-century concrete housing blocks are popularly known as *Mietkazernen* (rental barracks). Bruno Taut demands the dissolution of the cities in favour of expansive settlements where people will live from a natural exchange of its own products, so that even money will disappear. Travelling will cease to exist. No more hotels because everyone will have a room at home to take others in. The rule will be: 'Travel at home!' The urban landscape will disappear, too. Houses will be strewn about like grains of sand, fully supplied with natural gas and good lighting, with a choice of wallpaper designed to enhance illumination. Women will perform individual chores: looking after the children, cooking, serving meals, washing up, cleaning. Making the beds will be a task of all the members of the household, children included. Feather beds will be replaced with blankets. The nerve centre of the new settlement will be the kitchen. Family life will revolve around preparing and serving meals, clearing the table, washing up, going to bed, getting up, with a daily use of bath or wash-and-shower stall and closet. Churches will be erected in glass, illuminating the night.

In the simple logic of the new architects, the city is the symbol of state power. If the city disappears, politics too will cease to exist and there will be no more wars. 'You must be joking,' says the conservative right. What about the needs of Friedrich Nietzsche's *Ubermensch* (Superman) and the apotheosis of life through the industrial slaughter of war? War is a natural event! And by the way, walls made of glass are a nuisance because they cause a constant draught over the floor. The light is so blinding that it is impossible to sleep in those glass rooms. The gas flame of the gas stove is disrupted every time a door is opened. There is no place for storing wet coats, galoshes or umbrellas. Kitchen windows will be so high, that you will have to step onto the table to open them. 'Do not let anyone say anything against our old houses!' the conservatives cry out. 'What magnificent large rooms, bright staircases, giant corridors, endless landings. *Room* is what we have in these old houses. Admittedly, there are also bad-smelling toilets, but that doesn't matter: you don't have to spend too much time there if you don't want to. There is no bathroom in the old houses, but you do not have to bathe so often. Old houses make for much work, but in the old days the housewives knew no different and, remarkably, they still had time to raise a dozen children, cook wonderful food, and in between offer visitors coffee and fabulous bowls of punch. You have *time* to spare in the old houses.'

For the conservative right, 'modern' is just another word for 'asphalt democracy' – a phrase first used by a wandering, lovesick and club-footed adolescent from the town of Riehen near Cologne or, as Moeller van den Bruck phrases it, 'the mechanical democracy'.

His own books earn him next to nothing, and Moeller van den Bruck is constantly borrowing money. His only steady source of income has been his Dostoyevsky translations, a mammoth task, but that has come to an end, too. In 1922, the last of 22 volumes has been published.

Hedda is married to Herbert Eulenberg, a dramatist at the Deutsches Theater in Berlin and the Louise Dumonts Theater in Düsseldorf. They lived for some time in a new house in the Mecklenburgische-Strasse, in a desolate area opposite the railroad station; then they moved from Berlin to Düsseldorf with Moeller's almost adult son, Peter Wolfgang. Like his father, the young man is sad, full of melancholy, and withdrawn. For days on end, he refuses to speak.

Infrequently Moeller van den Bruck, who continuously rereads the letters friends have sent him in the past, receives a letter from Edvard Munch. The Norwegian artist has purchased the Ekely estate in Skoyen where he raises some cattle and grows fruit and vegetables in the fields surrounding his house. 'Death is the entry to life,' Munch writes in one of his letters. 'The more are destroyed, the more live.' Munch still paints variations of sexual attraction, love and melancholy in loneliness, but the obsessive repetition of the same theme and image has emptied compositions such as *The Scream*, *The Vampire* and *The Dance of Life* of their demonic power. He informs

Moeller van den Bruck that he has been commissioned to create paintings based on earlier compositions for a chocolate factory. Munch lives alone, enclosed in the environment of his bedroom, and yearns for peace of mind. Only a living room and his bedroom are furnished; all of the other rooms of the large estate at Ekely are given over to his paintings.

When Moeller van den Bruck receives a request from a well-wisher who asks the struggling author to comment on his earliest adolescent literary efforts, such as the few drama pieces for the theatre he wrote at the beginning of the century and two unfinished novels entitled *Colours of Autumn* and *Why this Song?* respectively – written at the time of the 'Schwarzen Ferkel' and the Society for Modern Art – he bitterly responds: 'May I ask you a favour? Please don't mention my earliest literature again.' Sometimes he gets some money from anonymous admirers in Berlin.

Moeller van den Bruck often feels ill. Attacks of rage come more and more frequently. Alcohol calms him down, at least in the morning when he feels dizzy. He starts the day with port wine, half a bottle. Port wine was the favourite drink of Edgar Allan Poe. Then some coffee and bread. By late afternoon, he becomes more and more agitated. Attacks, hallucinations; sometimes he has a whole day of vomiting. It takes him a couple of days to recover. His friends advise him to enter a sanatorium for medical treatment. Against his better judgement, Moeller van den Bruck still ignores the possibility of congenital syphilis, although he should know the symptoms: he is surely aware that Friedrich Nietzsche, whose writings he has studied and commented upon for over 20 years, died of the mental and physical ravages in the third and last stage of syphilis. Furthermore, he has read the 1919 American edition of Somerset Maugham's *The Moon and Sixpence* that paints a familiar picture of a syphilitic victim that slides into complete physical and mental breakdown.

Friedrich Nietzsche's madness came abruptly, unexpectedly, shortly after Christmas Eve, when he was barely 44 years of age. Nietzsche was writing a letter to the Swedish playwright August Strindberg and signed it at the bottom, 'Nietzsche Caesar'. Recognizing the disturbing signs, Strindberg fashioned a reply entirely in Greek and Latin. Nietzsche was living in Turin at that time. On the morning of 3 January 1889, upon leaving his lodgings, he saw a cab driver beating his horse in the Piazza Carlo Alberto. Tearfully, the philosopher flung his arms around the horse's neck; then he collapsed. He was carried back to his room. After lying motionless on a sofa for a while, he became boisterous and started singing, shouting and thumping at the piano. He wrote confused letters and signed them, 'The Crucified'. Nietzsche is interned at Dr Wille's clinic in Basel.

Released from the clinic, he went to live with his mother, then with his sister Elisabeth Foster-Nietzsche in Weimar. Elisabeth had lived in South America where she tried to establish an Aryan colony in the subtropical Paraguayan savanna. Nietzsche started speaking of himself as successor of the dead God; he wanted to address the crowds and shake everybody's hands. He claimed to be a famous man, and asked for women all the time. One morning, he started to undress on the pavement, in order to take a bath in a rain puddle. When the stroke came, Nietzsche sank back and died.

Moeller van den Bruck is not even 50, hardly a

middle-aged man. He doesn't complain, though, following the edict of Nietzsche that complaining is always useless and always a sign of weakness. In the sober, dull and tormented man who has abandoned art and literature for the world of politics and political machinations, his few friends of long-standing do not recognize the careless, carefree and wandering bohemian from his Paris years and the time he spent in Italy.

The pianist and composer Conrad Ansorge remarks in desperation: 'Moeller, I think you were born a married man!' Moeller van den Bruck is not interested in women, not anymore. At times, he becomes almost effeminate. The feminine use of his delicate hands and the way he carries himself makes observers at the June-Club suspect him of being a homosexual. He has urinary difficulties. Formerly exacting about his dress, he appears unconcerned and careless. He becomes generous beyond his means.

One Monday evening, he invites all the members of the club to a lavish dinner in the Erdener Treppchen wine bar, although he is broke and penniless. When the bill comes Moeller van den Bruck, in shame, hands over his business card and disappears for weeks. He is not only a sad, but also a deeply disillusioned man. He knows very well he is a failure as a writer. The books he has published under his own name have failed to win him a readership, even in his own country. None of his books has been translated, and few are ever reviewed. His Dostoyevsky translations are successful not because of the innate quality of the translation itself, but obviously because the brooding poetic irrationalism of the Russian giant appeals to sensitive spirits in Germany, from the extreme left to the extreme right.

By 1922, 179,000 copies of the first volume have been sold. He resents the lack of appreciation, but accepts the fact that he is not the new Nietzsche, after all.

Moeller van den Bruck develops odd ideas, weird and grotesque, and bordering on the eccentric: industrial workmen have to share the gifts of nature such as felling trees, sowing grain, digging in gardens, harvesting cabbages, playing with children. Modern man has to become the new embodiment of the heroes of Nietzsche. Industrial society kills the spiritual harmony of individuals, therefore life has to be lived according to the laws of nature. Politically, it is Moeller van den Bruck's ultimate goal to assist in the creation of a United States of Europe dominated by a strong and healthy Germany as its most powerful state.

Throughout his anguish, he keeps working. He has started to translate some more Guy de Maupassant short stories for the last of his series of eight volumes. Hedda Maase effectively helps him with the translation. Translated fragments are sent back and forth by post between Berlin and Düsseldorf on an almost daily basis.

Some days, his face and hands are covered with ulcers. His doctor treats him with salvarsan and neo-salvarsan, a yellow powder that is commercially available under the patented trade name Neoarsphenamine. Salvarsan contains 20 per cent arsenicum and has extremely painful side effects coupled with vomiting, migraine and anxiety attacks. To mask his slurred speech, Moeller van den Bruck resorts to excessive drinking. Sometimes at night, his arms and legs feel numb. During the day, he limps a little. He asks his doctor for advice. 'You will have attacks more and more frequently,' the doctor says. 'Feet, arms, finally it will affect your brain.' Otto Strasser knows of a particular Dr Boeck in Oslo who cares for infectious syphilitics. Dr Boeck strongly believes that isolation rather than the available form of treatment is the right and proper way to deal with the infection.

Moeller van den Bruck doesn't want to hear about it. He vows that he has a mission in life: he wants to write an essay on blood and soil that will be a bible for posterity. In his new book, he will lash out at believers and non-believers alike, hail the mystique of the national ideal, and recommend the most violent dynamism in order to restore the true values of the eternal Reich. Moeller van den Bruck professes that it will be his magnum opus, the pinnacle of his life as an artist. He intends to write a Nietzschean-style book in which he will for once and for all establish his guidelines for the future and predict the coming of a new 'Thousand-Year Reich'.

A greedy gaiety hangs over Berlin like an intoxicating smog. An American businessman throws a handful of small change on the floor of a bar, shouting at the top of his voice that only naked women are allowed to pick up the money. Immediately the girls in the bar strip off their blouses, skirts and underwear and drop to their knees. The American laughs.

'What's wrong?' an older, heavy-set woman who is stripped naked asks the American. 'I have to work a whole day for one American penny. Money doesn't stink. Not dollars, anyway.'

The war is not over yet. In actual fact, the war has never been over. Germany is in a state of civil unrest. War veterans – young men still, in their late twenties – are preparing themselves to continue the fight. Soldiers who have come back from the battlefields consider themselves to be freedom fighters, 'camping temporarily in the cities built by the fathers they hate'. They are waiting for the sign to destroy these cities, and build their own houses on the ruins of the past. Fathers call their sons nihilists, and the sons are proud to be labelled as such. It makes them invincible, and utterly dangerous. Twelve thousand German Jews have lost their lives for the Fatherland. Jewish organizations like the Fatherland Association of Jewish Front Soldiers are created, while 'anti'-groups and movements such as the Dürer-Group, the Folk Art Movement, the Social-Christians, the radical Race-Anti-Semites, the People's Movement and the Youth Movement are promoting the idea of the revolution of the sons against their fathers. They are anti-Semitic, nihilistic, charlatanesque, arch-conservative and aggressive nationalist desperadoes who have chosen the way of politics rather than gangsterism because politics seems to offer greater rewards.

Anti-republican coalitions of war veterans like the *Stahlhelm* (Steel Helmet) get into their ragged uniforms again and become paramilitary fighting forces and political pressure groups. Their spiritual leader is Friedrich Nietzsche and their lifeblood is the lost war, the 'Father of all Things'. Voices rise, and shout: 'We had to lose the war to win our Nation!' If Germany had won the war, it would have been the end. Now, it is a new beginning. The seeds of eternal life are planted in the leftover compost of the lost war, as Nietzsche would have worded it. The armistice is not to be seen as a time of shame and defeat, but as the beginning of the revolution that will destroy the old regime. Age-old discrepancies – between 'the spirit' and 'the body', 'myself' and 'the world', 'idealism' and 'materialism' – become superfluous. The individual is the collective, and vice versa. There is no beginning and no end; and inside is outside. Life is Death, and Death is Life. No one is an individual any more; people are particles in the Universe of Man.

A retired schoolmaster who lives in obscurity in Munich finds a publisher for a book that becomes an instant worldwide best-seller. Its title is *The Decline of the West*. The author is Oswald Spengler. 'In the heart of the people,' he writes, 'the Weimar constitution is doomed.' In what he calls his morphology of world history, Spengler asserts that the West is on a downward curve such as that which involved the ruin of the Roman Empire and its civilization. Cosmos turns to chaos, and civilization reverts to barbarism. Urbanization and materialism lead to decay. Spengler predicts a coming phase of Caesarism and wars of extermination. Within two years, the book sells over 36,000 copies in Germany alone.

Moeller van den Bruck does not share the black pessimism of Oswald Spengler. He strongly believes in regeneration, in life after death. Oswald Spengler is a provincial professor, cut off from the real world; Moeller van den Bruck is an intellectual who has travelled the world. All the while, newly formed fighting units such as 'Viking', 'Oberland', 'Wehrwolf' and 'Stahlhelm' are mushrooming all over the ruins of Germany. They call for immediate action. Where is the new Messiah? War veteran Ernst Jünger is a propagandist for 'the satanical synthesis between nationalism and bolshevism'. He calls it National Bolshevism; in the eyes of Jünger, there is nothing satanical about it: National Bolshevism is an anti-ideology, Prussian-style, and everything 'anti' is good.

Again, Moeller van den Bruck does not agree. He is more impressed by the achievements of Mussolini and the Italian Fascists. For the arch-conservative Moeller van den Bruck, the Italian national revival can teach Germany a lesson. Italo-Fascism is contemporary nationalism, the ideal synthesis of 'left' and 'right'. He describes himself as a devoted follower of Gabriele d'Annunzio and of the Italian nationalist Enrico Corradini who as early as 1914 cornered the idea of *il socialismo nazionale*, or National Socialism, the socialism of the 'New Right', a pressure group of which Moeller van den Bruck is a devoted follower.

'National Socialism Italian-style' is against nationalism, against socialism, against Communism, against liberalism, while it is in favour of an aggressive Fascist government led by a strong man who will stand above all political parties because he mistrusts them all. A dictator, in other words, in a dictatorial state. That this state is to be a European Germany or even a global 'Imperium Germanicum' is obvious. Moeller van den Bruck predicts that the dictator who will lead the disillusioned and defeated front soldiers to victory needs to be a war veteran himself. He can see only one man in the whole of Germany who fits the description, as if he were tailor-made for the job: General Erich Ludendorff. A man with an iron fist, but also a man of compromise. The society in which he lives is degenerate and doom-laden. 'A true Germany must emerge!' Moeller van den Bruck argues.

In modern art, only the criminal, the ugly and the blasphemous are of interest. Such is the opinion of the 'New Right'. Illustrated magazines feature naked dancers and international gangsters, frequently shown in company with each other. Jazz is 'rotten Negro music'. There is little if any idealism left among the young. Instead of Goethe, they read thrillers. Edgar Wallace is a best-seller in translation. Instead of Wagner, they prefer American hit songs. Instead of Nietzsche, Josephine Baker wearing only a banana-skirt is the toast of Berlin.

The New Right chooses to ignore the fact that the loosening of family ties and sexual mores is characteristic of other countries too. They do not compare Berlin to London, Paris or New York but to Germany as it has been and should become again. Berlin is a Babel of money and fashion, and Germany's provincial cities have lost their quiet, calm, small-town atmosphere of intimate warmth and friendliness. The New Right rejects the cosmopolitan view of the universal metropolis. They see debris and waste everywhere and lament the monopolization of the world.

Like-minded critics are the philosopher Martin Heidegger and the novelist Stefan Zweig. Heidegger castigates urban life for its air of superficiality and absence of solitude. Stefan Zweig says that while Berlin is Americanized, his home town of Vienna is Budapested. Two or three decades earlier, one waltzed in Vienna, danced the csardas in Hungary and the bolero in Spain. Now everyone dances to the jazz band.

Modernism is the negation of German idealism. The German public has to be re-educated; it has to rediscover its national and cultural heritage. Not all literature written in the German language is perforce German literature since the work of Jewish writers does not belong to German literature. Theatre has lost out to cinema. New York decrees short hair for women?

Within a month, German women have their hair cut short. Stefan Zweig claims that since everything is geared to the shortest unit of time, as a consequence consumption increases and genuine education – the patient accumulation of knowledge over the course of a lifetime – becomes a rare phenomenon. What is not American, is given an American title. The libertine ballads of François Villon dating back to the French Middle Ages are published in German as 'songs'. The image of the German soldier running to his death with a copy of Goethe's *Faust* in his knapsack is thrown away with all the other war lies. Although they differ on details, the New Right joins the likes of Oswald Spengler and Ernst Jünger in calling for a 'conservative revolution', a 'revolution of the right' based on the old Teutonic desire for power and for plunder. The forces of the left wonder: 'But what *is* there to *conserve*?'

There are queues in front of the shops, and pale, patient faces everywhere. Women wear their kitchen dresses. Yesterday, rice cost 80,000 marks per pound. Today rice is priced at 160,000 marks. The man behind the counter shrugs his shoulders and says, 'No more rice.' Noodles, then. 'No more noodles.' The brand-new banknotes are still moist from the printers. They shrink in value on the way to the grocer's shop.

The shopkeeper laughs. 'Cheaper butter! Remember – 1,600,000 marks yesterday, just 1,400,000 marks today.'

The weekend markets overflow with people. City police regulate traffic.

'I'll have two dozen turnips.'

'There's only one dozen left.'

Instead of meat, bones are being sold. Shoppers swallow

the butcher's biting remark that every cow has to have a cadaver. They pay, and stagger off.

'Come on, when will I finally get my butter?'

'Your butter? By the time you get to the front of the queue all the butter will be gone!'

The policeman watching guard outside the shop pulls the sobbing woman from the store.

From midnight on, endless lines form outside the bank, all trying to be the first customer when the cash drawers open. Savers have been seized by panic. Their money is lost. No one makes deposits any more. All credits are called in. Lines in front of the banks grow longer. Banks cannot make repayments. Banking hours are limited to two hours a day, then to one hour. People who have been rich before are suddenly glad to have someone hand them a bowl of warm soup. Paper money starts selling by the pound. A 1 million mark banknote does not even buy a slice of bread. Pawn shops are doing a roaring trade.

Catastrophe is imminent, and everyone senses it.

The Jewish author Ephraim Frisch, a consultant to various publishing houses in Berlin, naively writes: 'The final myth Europe still possesses, is the myth of the Jew. Europe obviously does not want to see its Jews destroyed.' The Scheunenviertel in Berlin is populated with large numbers of Jews from eastern Europe who have fled to Germany to escape Russian and Polish persecution. Berlin-based Joseph Roth, a journalist, writes that no eastern Jew has come to Berlin voluntarily. He asks the unanswered question: 'Who in the whole world would come to Berlin voluntarily?' Most eastern Jews are in Berlin on a transit visa, authorizing them to stay for two or three days. They stay for two to three years before travelling to Amsterdam, or to America. For most of them, their identity documents are not in order, or they are false documents, often from family members who have died or stayed behind in Russia or Poland. They do not register with the police, since the Berlin police has the habit of checking up on people in their houses. Eastern Jews have no licence to trade; they stand on the corner of Joachimsthaler-Strasse and Kurfürstendamm and buy old clothes from passers-by. Then they have the clothes mended, freshened up, and ironed. For a small profit, they sell them at the clothes market. There are only a couple of Jewish streets in the Scheunenviertel and around the Warschauer Bridge.

The most Jewish of all Berlin streets is the Hirten-Strasse, the 'sad Hirten-Strasse', in the words of Joseph Roth. There are no trams running along the sad street, and rarely an automobile. Always trucks, and most of the time hand-drawn barrows. Down at the bottom of some narrow steps, little Jewish taverns are sited in the wall. There is always rubbish in the doorways: old newspapers, soles and shoes, small pieces of used furniture; rubbish that has been collected in Greater Berlin to be resold. A Jewish bakery sells poppy-seed bagels, rolls, black bread. There is a synagogue for Jews with prayer shawls, their *tefillin*. In the back room of the small taverns, they drink the Jewish national drink, mead, made by fermenting honey and water. Heavy, dark brown mead. It is sweet, bitter and powerful. They all have some bread and an onion in one pocket, because who knows if they will not have to resume their wanderings at any hour? Lunch consists of bread and sausages.

In the courtyard of a tavern, with a linden tree in the

middle, a theatre is set up. Hebrew and Yiddish poems of Jewish authors are recited. Under the rustle of the linden leaves, the musicians sing the melodies from the east:

> Unter die grune Beimelach
> sizzen die Mojschelach, Schlojmelach,
> Eugen wie gliehende Keulalach . . .

> Under the little green tree
> sit the Moishes, the Shlomos,
> Eyes like glowing coal . . .

The musicians – a choir of six men – are the six sons of the great Mendel from Bericzew, whom only the oldest Jews can still remember. His violin playing was so splendid, that no one could ever forget it, not in Lithuania, in Volynka nor in Galicia. Once one has heard this painful song that 'smiles beneath the tears', a song so full of melancholy that its pain floats all over Europe, it echoes for weeks and weeks.

The Third Reich

The idea of party leadership crops up, inspired by the example of Lenin and Trotsky in Russia, and Mussolini in Italy. Hermann Esser, party member number two and the man who chairs most of the party's meetings, proclaims: 'We need not spend much time looking for a German Mussolini; we have him already and his name is Adolf Hitler.' Hitler takes over the leadership of the party. More and more, he assumes the appearance of a character out of a painting by Franz von Stuck, *The Wild Chase*, painted in the year of Hitler's birth. The lock of hair, the moustache and the Wagnerian drama are all there. Hitler's favourite painting by Franz von Stuck is the *Medusa*. He is fascinated by it. When he first saw a reproduction in an art book, he exclaimed: 'Those eyes are the eyes of my mother!' Hitler is so sensitive about his appearance, that he has himself photographed in new outfits to study their effect before appearing in them in public. He examines himself in a mirror and asks if he looks the part of the Führer.

Rudolf Hess joins the party. Hitler fondly calls him *mein Rudi*. Hitler orders Hess to set up a card index on the weaknesses and potential dangers of all his followers and early party members. Hess is studying economy at Munich University, under the guidance of Karl Haushofer, whose son is a member of the June-Club in Berlin. As a former army lieutenant, Hess attends classes dressed in a field-grey uniform with the Nazi

Party badge and the orange lion of the Free Corps on his sleeve. Hess and Karl Haushofer are associates of the intensely anti-Semitic Thule Society, a magical brotherhood that derives its name from one of the early lost continents, like Lemuria and Atlantis. The Thule Society is interested in Nordic mythology and political conspiracy. Other members of the Thule Society who proudly wear the Nazi Party badge are Karl Harrer and Alfred Rosenberg, the party philosopher. Hess writes to his mother in Reicholdgrün: 'Every day I am with Hitler. A splendid man.' One week later: 'Received a long letter from General Ludendorff about the party. He asks for discretion.' The following year: 'Berlin Jews hold the limelight. What is Hitler going to do?'

Hitler travels to Berlin to get in touch with the national elements in the Reich capital. He wants to assess the possibility of carrying the Nazi movement beyond Bavaria into the rest of Germany, and he can use any support he can get in Berlin. Hitler also intends to monitor the People's Freedom Party, one of several small right-wing groups in the capital that share similar nationalist views to those advocated by the Nazi Party in Munich.

In Berlin, Hitler stays at the home of the Bechsteins, patriotic and extremely wealthy piano manufacturers. Their Jewish-sounding name does not frighten Hitler. The Bechstein family are old friends of Dietrich Eckart, and the latter has presented his political pupil to them. Helene Bechstein introduces Hitler to her social circle. His thin, pale face is seen by most women as tragic. Helene Bechstein says she wishes that Hitler was her son. Hitler sits at her feet. She gently strokes his hair. '*Mein Wölfchen*,' she murmurs tenderly, 'my little Wolf.' Frau Bechstein is 20 years older than Hitler. Family friends

believe that Helene Bechstein is grooming Hitler in the
expectation that he will one day marry her daughter
Lottie, who is far from attractive. Hitler does once
propose to Lottie, but is refused. When moving in this
milieu, Hitler changes into a modest, shy, almost clumsy
man, who relaxes only when he starts to pontificate about
Richard Wagner. At the house of the Bechsteins, Hitler
takes speech lessons in order to remedy his Austrian
accent and strengthen his voice. He extends his stay in
Berlin to six weeks. On his return to Munich, Hitler
recalls his visit to Berlin to his friends Putzi Hanfstäengl
and Dietrich Eckart: 'When I went to Berlin a few weeks
ago and looked at the traffic on the Kurfürstendamm,
the luxury, the perversion and the Jewish materialism
disgusted me so thoroughly, that I was almost beside
myself. I nearly imagined myself to be Jesus Christ when
He came to the temple and found it taken in by the
money-changers. I can well imagine how He felt when
He seized a whip and scourged them out.'

The Berlin newspapers report that Corporal Hitler
is fiercely moving forward with the Nazi Party's 25
point programme. Rudolf Pechel, the publisher of the
Deutsche Rundschau, who is an active member of the
June-Club, invites Hitler to one of the Monday evening
gatherings of the club in order to clarify the Nazi Party's
political profile, followed by debate.

In his speech, Hitler claims that he and his supporters
were the first to declare that the Versailles Treaty was
a crime. He continues: 'With the armistice began the
humiliation of Germany. If the leaders of the Weimar
Republic on the day of its foundation would have said to
the country, "Germans, stand together! The Fatherland

expects you to fight to your last breath!", then millions who are now enemies of Weimar would be fanatical republicans. Today we are the enemies of the republic not because it is a republic but because this republic is founded on the humiliation of the Fatherland. It was no Treaty of Peace which was signed, but a betrayal of peace.' He explains the first and fundamental task of the National Socialist movement: 'Make Germany once more National, so that the Fatherland shall stand above everything else. Teach our people the truth of the old saying: He who will not be a hammer must be the anvil. Today we are the anvil, and out of the anvil we will fashion once more a hammer, and a German sword.' Hitler reveals himself as the enemy of the democratic order and of the Versailles Treaty with which the Weimar Republic is associated. The Weimar Republic had been born in troubled times, and it faces a troubled future. It represents a middle way between the nationalism on the right and socialism and Communism on the left. Hitler says that way is doomed. 'There are only two possibilities for Germany,' he remarks. 'The people will turn to the left, and then God help us! for it will lead to complete destruction. Or else the party of the right will ruthlessly seize power, and that will be the beginning of the German renaissance.'

Hitler's appearance at the June-Club is not a runaway success. The Berlin intellectuals are harbouring doubts. Hitler senses mistrust. After his speech, he shakes hands with Moeller van den Bruck and apologizes for his rather weak performance. 'I am but a drummer,' he says. 'I can drum support, but I am not the potential leader of a National Socialist authoritarian state. I am but a propagandist for the national cause.'

Heinrich Brüning, a Catholic lawyer, protests loudly.

'But you,' Hitler says to Moeller van den Bruck, 'you have everything I lack. You can create the spiritual framework for Germany's reconstruction. Otto Strasser whose advice I rate highly says that you are the Jean-Jacques Rousseau of the German revolution. A born thinker. I am a street fighter. Join us! If you can become the Jean-Jacques Rousseau of the New Germany, I will be its Napoleon. Let us work together!'

Among the small crowd in the bodega are two former warlords, imperial navy Admiral Ludwig von Schröder and infantry General Oskar von Hutier, wartime commander of the 18th Army in which Rudolf Hess served. They urge Moeller van den Bruck to accept Hitler's proposal straight away, no strings attached.

Moeller van den Bruck is still sceptical. To Heinrich Brüning, he says: 'I would rather commit suicide than see such a man in office. With Hitler at the helm, our nation of poets and philosophers is bound to become a nation of criminals and murderers.' Then he spots his friend Rudolf Pechel, who introduced Hitler to the June-Club. Moeller van den Bruck rests his hand on Pechel's shoulder, and says, 'Pechel, that friend of yours, Hitler, doesn't understand us. Let's forget about him and go to the bodega for another bottle of Spanish wine.' Moeller van den Bruck then turns to Otto Strasser, and says: 'Hitler is a catastrophe!'

The next day, both the imperial navy admiral and the infantry general enlist in Hitler's Nazi Party.

Russian emigrants with no clear reason to stay, start to return to Paris or leave for Prague. A great portion of the artistic community in Berlin has little to eat.

Handouts are not disdained. The bohemian is dead, or he has already left the city. Vladimir Nabokov finds himself a job in Berlin's booming film industry. The starlets call him 'the English prince' because he always wears a blazer with the Cambridge escutcheon on its breast pocket. The novel is dead, because people lack time to read. Painting and sculpture are dead; in an age of photography and film, they seem a waste of time and effort. *L'art pour l'art* – art for art's sake – is dead. Piet Mondrian is considered the best of 'individual' artists. The elegant life is blown out of the modern city. Berlin is the amusement capital of the world.

Behind the revolving doors of the Romanisches Café, Egon Erwin Kirsch reads the newspapers, rubbing shoulders with the art dealers Flechtheim and Cassirer, the most influential and important art dealers in Berlin at that time. Cassirer is the exclusive dealer of expressionist sculptor Ernst Barlach, and of Max Beckmann. Without the coffee-house, one cannot live. 'You telephone your friends, make an appointment in a coffee-house, and the wheel of intellectual and social conversation comes full circle,' says Kirsch. They drink mocha and discuss Picasso, Mussolini, Sarotti (a popular brand of chocolate), works of art and big deals. The daily speciality in the Romanisches Café is a soft-boiled egg served in a glass. The illustrator Rudolf Grossmann invents the 'sport' of drawing without looking at the paper. The artist Richard Orlik even makes a drawing on a piece of paper hidden in his trouser pocket.

The smaller back room of the Romanisches Café is known as 'the swimming-pool'. This is where the artists gather. Here Bertolt Brecht, Billy Wilder, Heinrich and Thomas Mann, Joseph Roth and Carl Zuckmayer meet

Sinclair Lewis who comes from abroad. The title 'artist' becomes an insult. A Russian art exhibition is held at the Lutz Gallery exhibiting works by Kandinsky, Chagall, Malevich, Rodchenko, Tatlin and El Lissitzky. The artists themselves refer to their paintings as 'production art'.

In a Berlin museum, a bullet is fired, damaging a Rubens painting. With a cry of joy, war veteran artist George Grosz shouts: 'We welcome the news that bullets are whistling through the art galleries and into the masterpieces of Rubens rather than into the houses of the poor in the working-class neighbourhoods.' Dadaist artists ask to exchange museum pictures for food supplies with the Allies. Modern artists claim that the cleaning of a gun is of greater significance than the entire metaphysical output of all the old masters together.

Twenty-year-old Maria Magdalene von Losch plays the violin in a cabaret orchestra at night; by day she works in a glove factory, a hat shop and a newspaper kiosk. She wears bright red hats with long feathers and wears lacquered shoes, although she lives in Spartan lodgings. When Maria Magdalene von Losch lands her first film role in *Der kleine Napoleon* (The little Napoleon), a historical costume drama about the amorous adventures of Napoleon's younger brother, she immediately changes her name to Marlene Dietrich.

An 18-year-old Swedish girl named Greta Gustafsson comes to Berlin to attend the German première of her first film, *The Story of Gösta Berling*, a four-hour epic directed by Mauritz Stiller, the greatest film-maker in Sweden. *Gösta Berling* is a critical and commercial success. Day after day, the large UFA-Palast with several thousand seats is sold out. Louis B. Mayer, one of the vice-presidents of Hollywood film company MGM, is travelling through Berlin. He sees *Gösta Berling* and is impressed. He decides that Greta Gustafsson should work for him in Hollywood. He offers her a contract for three years. She will earn 400 dollars a week for the first year, 600 dollars a week for the second and 750 dollars a week for the third year. Greta Gustafsson doesn't speak any English, but that doesn't matter. After all, it is silent film. While she is in Berlin, she stars in a film called *Street without Joy* and changes her name to Greta Garbo.

Three young Berliners place a sound track directly on a film. Their first sound picture stars chickens in a barnyard. Berlin film studios reject the innovation. Films are not supposed to talk. The painter Max Liebermann is having a mocha with friends in the Romanisches Café. He is 70, and a famous man. Max Liebermann is one of the original German Impressionists. He is also a cousin of Walther Rathenau. Marlene Dietrich in her lacquered shoes strolls past the Romanisches Café. Max Liebermann turns to his table companions and sighs: '. . . Oh, to be 50 years younger!'

Doom philosophers who still believe that the war has been fought to protect *Kultur* against the threat of *Zivilisation* are powerless against the lure of luxury. Those who have survived the bloodshed of the war do not embrace the pessimism of the intellectual conservative élite. They fancy the fashionable lifestyle that brings them American jazz and American dances such as the charleston and the shimmy. All traditional aristocratic notions of culture inherent in the old political system are called into question.

In the press, America is held up as the cultural model

of the future. The figures are staggering: over 4,000 titles – daily broadsheets, tabloids and magazines – are published in Germany. Berlin alone has 45 morning papers, 2 lunch-time papers and 14 evening papers. The illustrated press actively promotes a new way of life that is easy, forward-looking and fun-filled. The monthly *Uhu* (Owl) and *The Lady* are devoted to the image of the 'new women'. Market leader among fashion magazines is the German edition of *Vogue*. *Der Querschnitt* (Cross-section) is the German answer to *The New Yorker*. Some of the weekly magazines such as the *Berliner Illustrierte Zeitung* (Berlin Illustrated News), known as *BIZ*, reach circulations of over 1 million. The *BIZ* introduces the photo-essay, a new journalistic form in which several pages of photographs are devoted to a single topic. It publishes pictures of Caesar, Napoleon, Lenin, Ataturk in Turkey, Mussolini in Italy and Primo de Rivera in Spain. 'In chaotic Europe,' writes the *Berliner Illustrierte Zeitung*, 'there is a growing belief in the dictator as Messiah.'

In his review of *Federicus Rex*, the film critic Curt Rosenberg asks: 'Where lies the power of this film? In the appearance of the great king, who is the primal image of the strong man for whom so many long today?' Hitler postpones a conference to see the film, in which Frederick the Great beheads his own son. He is entranced.

In this international melting pot of fun, fantasy and hard reality a young man from the Rhineland with a ravenous sexual appetite is trying to find his way. He is 25 years of age, and he intends to become a writer. He has written an autobiographical novel entitled *Michael*. All the publishers in Berlin have turned his manuscript down, but they haven't been able to discourage him.

He is writing two plays: *The Wanderer*, about the life of Jesus Christ, and *The Lonesome Guest*. Both are in verse. No producer he has contacted will stage either of the two plays. He submits dozens of articles to the liberal daily *Berliner Tageblatt* (Berlin Daily News); none is ever published. His application for a reporter's job has been turned down.

He is a short and slim man with a club foot. When he was four, he contracted infantile paralysis; his growth was retarded and the paralysis permanently affected his foot. He walks with a noticeable limp. On the grounds of his physical inferiority, he is rejected for army service. His name is Joseph Goebbels. His mother is of Dutch origin. He worked for eight or nine months as a minor bank clerk at the Cologne branch of the Dresdner Bank; then he took a job at the Cologne Stock Exchange calling out the position of shares. When he was fired from his job, he started drifting through Germany, first to Heidelberg, then to Munich, and finally Berlin.

A voracious reader, he also writes for hours every day – letters, diary entries, reflections, whatever. In a Christmas letter to his girlfriend Else he laments: 'The world has turned itself into a mad-house. Some of the best men are prepared to join the obscene dance round the golden calf. New times, so they say, demand new men. I cannot join them.' In another letter to Else he calls himself 'un-modern'. He has a sharp tongue, maybe because he has been an amateur actor in his school days. When he runs out of money, he coldly notes in his diary: '*Ich habe kein Geld* (I don't have any money).' A few days later: '*Geldnot!* (Lack of money).' His diary is a record of his life meant not for publication but for his own eyes only. It is composed in the form of notes, mixed with the occasional quotation from Goethe's *Faust*.

In a pawnshop he sells his watch, to a Jew. He reads Ibsen, Thomas Mann, Tolstoy and the Piper-Verlag edition of Dostoyevsky's *The Brothers Karamazov*, a passionate drama of family rivalry, in the translation of Moeller van den Bruck and Lucy Kaerrick. Then he reads Richard Wagner's *Mein Leben* (My Life). Soon Joseph Goebbels runs out of money again. '*Was nun?* he asks his diary. What now? He provides the answer himself: '*Bei den Arbeitslosen.*' The dole. He wants to write a novel using his own love letters for inspiration. In his diary he writes: 'I'm waiting for Else. My heart beats like mad. Eros! Eros!! Eros!!!' He reads Dostoyevsky's short story *Netotschka Neswanowa*. His first impressions are jotted down in his diary: 'Loved it. Psychology of Russians is so simple. Russia holds the key to a European solution.' Then Goebbels reads Rosa Luxemburg's *Prison Letters to Karl Liebknecht* and writes down, 'Perhaps an idealist'. He mentions that he feels a warm sympathy towards Rosa Luxemburg and Karl Liebknecht.

In a moment of despair, he opens his heart onto the blank pages of his diary: 'My future is in the dark. I fear everything. I've got nothing to long for. Nothing to look forward to when I wake up in the morning. I live from day to day. All roads are closed. Where do I find salvation?' Ten days later: 'Everything I undertake fails.' He fears he has tuberculosis when he has a pain in his back.

Undaunted by previous refusals, Joseph Goebbels sends a new letter of application for work to the liberal *Berliner Tageblatt*. He asks for a salary of 250 marks a month and a job on the editorial staff. Once more, he is rejected. He approaches Karl Kaufmann, the regional leader of the Nazi Party for the Rhine–Ruhr district, and offers his services. Kaufmann discusses the matter with Gregor Strasser who is thinking of producing a small weekly journal. They will need an editorial assistant. Otto Strasser has been appointed editor of the journal, and he arranges with Kaufmann to interview Goebbels for the position. 'We are going to win the German working people for National Socialism. We are going to destroy Marxism!' Goebbels says fiercely, in an attempt to convince Strasser that he is the man he's looking for. 'We shall sweep bourgeois Germany into the dustbin!' Strasser is impressed. He engages Goebbels as editorial assistant and to help with secretarial work for the northern party organization. His liaison man in Munich is another young man whose time has yet to come: Heinrich Himmler.

Moeller van den Bruck has moved from an impressive house in the Holsteinische-Strasse 31 to a small villa located at Unter den Eichen 127, in the green suburban district of Berlin-Steglitz. It will be his last address. His rooms are dim and damp, and very darkly curtained in purple velvet. What light there is, is stained by Gallé glass lamps. The master of the house strides through the darkened rooms dressed in a velvet evening gown.

The walls of the house are lined with books, and any wall space left over is taken up by paintings, drawings and framed etchings. Moeller van den Bruck owns various paintings by the Dutch Impressionist, pointillist and symbolist Jan Toorop, an artist friend of Charles Rennie Mackintosh, as well as several pen-and-ink drawings by Aubrey Beardsley. His pride and joy are

the series of five coloured etchings entitled *Les Sataniques*
(*The Bedevilled*) by the Belgian symbolist Félicien
Rops, who lived in Paris. Not only was Rops a friend of
Baudelaire, he also successfully illustrated Jules Barbey
d'Aurevilley's novel *Les Diaboliques* (*The Possessed*)
which had been translated by Moeller van den Bruck and
published in three volumes in 1900. The Rops etchings
depict Satan as the Devil, the 'Master over Sexuality'. In
one of the etchings, Satan throws a feast of naked women
over Paris. At one time, Moeller van den Bruck owned a
Munch painting, executed with thinned oil paint slashed
onto raw canvas and completed shortly before Munch
left for Weimar to carry out the task of creating a large,
symbolic portrait of Friedrich Nietzsche, but he had to
sell the painting to cover his mounting debt. Some of the
cubist-like massive bronzes by his sculptor friend Ernst
Barlach, which are displayed throughout the house, owe
their inspiration to the art of Africa and the South Seas.

Surrounded with the memories of his life, his books,
his paintings, letters, notebooks, manuscripts, empty wine
bottles, pill boxes, magazines and periodicals, yellowed
newspapers, fragments of his unfinished autobiography
and a large death mask of Napoleon on black silk,
Moeller van den Bruck dips his pen in ink and starts
writing his *magnum opus* in praise of the 'Thousand-Year
Reich'.

Once a monocled dandy and a 'disillusioned aesthete',
Moeller van den Bruck has become an agitator on paper.
In a letter to Friedrich Schweiss he explains the reasons
for his transformation from a literary bohemian to a
political commentator: 'My aim in life was to become a
German Plutarch. A literary biographer of exceptional
quality. But when I was living in Paris, life overtook

literature. As a German living abroad, I sensed that we stood on the eve of a confrontation between France and Germany. That is the reason why I wrote *The Germans*: to boost German morale.' In a letter to Hans Grimm, he writes: 'Although we lost the war, our nation is the moral victor.'

Moeller van den Bruck is living in a Utopian, 'revolutionary' Germany, a Germany that no longer exists. His criticism of the political system and his analysis of it is purely destructive. Political parties are Germany's misfortune. Whoever destroys them by fire and sword will be doing a noble deed. Strong leadership is natural, whereas parliamentary discussion is artificial and undesirable. Moeller van den Bruck writes his ultimate attack on liberalism in a hypnotic state, as if in a trance. It is a painstakingly methodical and disciplined manuscript full of contrasting poetic visions, enormous prophecies and declarations and apocalyptic predictions. He takes endless pains to polish his sentences, to such an extent that his writing becomes tortuous – twisted and obscure. In broad strokes, Moeller van den Bruck paints the glorious history of the First and Second Reich, both long gone. Again and again, throughout the centuries, there has arisen in Germany some ruler who succeeded temporarily in bringing together the scattered Germanic people under one banner. Uniting all the German states in one Reich has therefore been a dominant feature of German patriotism and statesmanship for centuries.

First there was Clovis, at the end of the fifth century. At the close of the eighth century, Charlemagne established a wide hegemony in Europe. Otto I asserted himself as the German king over five great duchies – Saxony, Franconia, Thuringia, Swabia and Bavaria – and was crowned Emperor of the Holy Roman Reich by the Pope in Rome in the year 962. Their status as Holy Roman emperors drew the German kings across the Alps to assert their claims in Italy. The Rhine was no longer a frontier, as it had been in Roman times, for German territories stretched far to the west and south.

Frederick II, the white-haired 'small and ugly' Holy Roman emperor, son of the paranoid Henry of Swabia or Henry IV and grandson of Barbarossa, conquered Jerusalem in 1228, during the Crusades to recover the Holy City for Christendom. His erudition, love of the arts and court splendour earned him the title *Stupor Mundi*, Wonder of the World. He died at the age of 56 on 13 December 1250, having ruled a large part of Europe, uniting north and south, and stood for tolerance, multicultural pluralism and federalism. He is hailed as a precursor of modern European integration.

The Teutonic Knights, originally a crusading order, conquered East Prussia. Under Emperor Charles V (1519–56), the vast empire included Austria, the Netherlands, Spain and part of the New World. By war and inheritance, Frederick the Great (1740–86) acquired a chain of territories stretching from the Polish frontiers westwards to the Rhine. A sovereign ruler by God's grace, Frederick the Great built an efficient military state, with a powerful army. It was said that Prussia was not a country with an army, but an army with a country.

In 1760 the Russians entered Berlin, and in 1806 the French troops under Napoleon marched in triumph into the German capital. The Holy Roman Empire known as the First Reich came to an end. In 1862, Bismarck came to power as minister-president of Prussia. He immediately set himself the task of destroying liberalism in order to strengthen conservative Prussia and maintain her position as a great power. In the process, he reunited Germany. As a youth, Bismarck fought some 25 duels. As a man, he engineers three wars. 'The great questions of the day,' Bismarck said, 'are not settled by resolutions and majority votes but by blood and iron.' Bismarck taught the German people to consider lack of morality as the quality of a great statesman. In Germany under Bismarck, power is idealized, war is made heroic and the national idea is absolute, while the belief in the superiority of the Aryan or Teutonic race is overemphasized. In the 1870–1 Franco-Prussian war, Prussia defeats France. Wilhelm I becomes the German emperor and the Second Reich is proclaimed in Louis XIV's magnificent palace at Versailles.

For Moeller van den Bruck there is no doubt that again the arch-enemy of German culture is liberalism, which stands for everything that is corrupt. He acknowledges that the Weimar Republic is revolutionary, but he does not accept its revolution. He aims at a new revolution, one that eliminates the residue of the French Revolution and restores 'eternal values', without which man loses contact with nature and with God. 'The Father of Nationalism is War,' Moeller van den Bruck writes with pomp. Life has to be a struggle of wills, in which individuals and movements are in constant conflict. The confused and weak Weimar democracy with its powerless government and quarrelling politicians can only be erased and replaced by the revolution of the right that will bring order, discipline and efficiency. The real enemy is not the 'Red Republic' in Russia, but the Weimar Republic at home. The war of 1914 had been the result of the slow unravelling of the old economic and cultural principles. Reconstruction can only be brought about on the basis of a new order which will re-establish harmony between capital and labour, between the individual and the community, between the people and their religion, between man and God.

Moeller van den Bruck suggests that the conservatives should borrow heavily from socialism to create a new, German socialism – a National Socialism, or better still, a German Fascism. His boundless admiration for Mussolini and all things Italian is evident. 'The Italian people,' he applauds, 'live in freedom, independence and unity. The Germans do not.' Which leads him to the conclusion that 'the Italian Fascists have turned Italy into a State that hitherto only existed in poetry.' The German people have no 'today', only a 'yesterday' and perhaps a 'tomorrow'. 'We have to be strong to live in contradictions,' writes Moeller van den Bruck. Humans have to be controlled, like machines.

Liberalism is incapable of solving the problems of modern mass society. The shortcomings of the Weimar Republic are the logical outcome of an unsuitable political order. He writes: 'Liberalism has undermined cultures, destroyed religions and the Fatherland. It is decomposition, the self-surrender of mankind.'

It is not true that a profound cultural crisis has placed the West in an 'iron cage' of modernization from which escape is all but impossible, argues Moeller van den Bruck. There is a way out – the new society he has in mind; a society injected with the vitality of Nietzsche. On almost every page of his manuscript, he praises his love for Nietzsche 'who stands at the opposite pole of thought to Marx'. 'Nietzsche,' says Moeller van den Bruck, 'knew that democracy is only the superficial phenomenon of a dying society.' The way out of the abyss is this new society, this new Reich that will be an empire of organization and discipline in the midst of European chaos. A Reich in which the First Reich and Bismarck's 'In between Reich' merge with the Second Reich into a 'Final Reich' in which there is no distinction any more between the eternal political opponents of left and right, of socialism and nationalism. A Final Reich that is the personification not of God the Father, not of God the Son, but of God the Holy Spirit; a Final Reich that is governed not by the political parties of the left nor those of the right, but by a third political movement: the Party of the Third Reich.

Moeller van den Bruck concludes: 'We believe that it is the mission of the German nation to translate the world revolution into the salvation of Europe. The world revolution will not be what Marx envisaged; it will be the one Nietzsche foresaw.' He expresses his hope that a saviour, a Führer, will arise to lead Germany out of its present misery to a better, brighter future. In his last chapter, Moeller van den Bruck writes: 'It is nowhere written that a people have a right to eternal life. No more glorious end could be conceived for a great people than to perish in a World War. The thought of enduring peace is the thought of the Third Reich. But it must be fought for.'

The book is written in a biting, aggressive, offensive, militant and at times vulgar and lethal language: 'Our Second Reich was a Little-German Reich because it did not include Austria; we must consider it only as a stepping stone on our path to a Greater-German Reich. The Second Reich was only the transition to a Third

Reich, a new and final Reich for which we must live, *if we are to live at all.*

In the fall of 1922, the German government asks the Allies to grant a moratorium on reparations payments. Germany claims it cannot go on paying. The French government bluntly refuses. As if it were a sign of providence, Germany defaults in deliveries of timber at the time when Moeller van den Bruck is ready to bring his new manuscript to his publisher. French and Belgian troops are moved in and occupy the Ruhr Valley, an area containing four-fifths of Germany's resources in coal and iron. Systematically, they begin to confiscate the country's coal reserves. Blood flows in the streets. French policy is to stay there until Germany decides to pay up. The Nazis are rallying in Berlin's Sportpalast. Thomas Mann calls Hitler 'a foreign vagabond'. Alsace-Lorraine reverts to France. Military conscription is strictly prohibited. The collapse of Germany's economy in the Ruhr Valley hastens the final plunge of the mark. It falls to 17,972 marks to the dollar. The Weimar government deliberately lets the mark tumble, since the inflation also wipes out the war debt.

Amidst the political turmoil, *The Third Reich* is published by Ring-Verlag in Berlin with a first printing of 20,000 copies. It is a 263-page book and costs 5 marks only. At the last moment, Moeller van den Bruck inserts a preface which is an open letter to Heinrich von Gleichen, one of the co-founders of the June-Club.

Dear Gleichen,

This book is addressed to Germans of every party. Instead of government by party, I offer the ideal of the Third Reich. It is an old German concept and a great one. It arose when our First Reich fell; it was accelerated by the thought of a Thousand-Year Reich, but its underlying concept is the dawn of a German age, in which the German people would for the first time fulfil their destiny on earth. The Third Reich is a philosophical idea not for this but for the next world. *Germany might perish because of the Third Reich dream.*

Signed: MOELLER VAN DEN BRUCK
January 1923

The word 'Reich' means realm, kingdom – the kingdom not only of politics and governments, but in addition the kingdom of the spirit. 'Reich' is also a German form of the Latin word 'Regnum'. Thus Moeller van den Bruck's Third Reich suggests analogies with Dostoyevsky's 'Third Rome', and these analogies – passionate, prophetic, transfused in blood, with all the mystic associations which adhere to the word 'Reich' with its torch-like quality – have coloured his thinking and his writing. *The Third Reich* is written in an almost impenetrable 'Prussian style', which Moeller van den Bruck has worked out for himself on the Nietzschean model. While he has been writing his magnum opus, Moeller van den Bruck's only son Peter Wolfgang, 21 years of age, has died of pneumonia.

30 April 1923: 'Orders have come in from Munich. Tonight we attack!' Heinrich Himmler says.

For weeks, Hitler has been declaring at numerous party meetings that the Reds will have to trample over his dead body if they want to demonstrate in Munich on 1 May, Labour Day. Heinrich Himmler stands at attention in the chemist's shop of Gregor Strasser. He is an unemployed agriculturist who hopes to become an army officer.

'Orders from Hitler?' asks Gregor Strasser.

'Yes,' Himmler says.

A counter-demonstration is to be attempted under the military leadership of General Ludendorff. At nightfall Gregor Strasser's army of 3,000 Storm Troopers marches off from Landshut. The veteran soldiers are dressed in their old field-grey war uniforms, with brown shirts and swastika's everywhere. A small number of lorries lit by kerosene lanterns has been put at their disposal.

It is a pitch-black night. Suddenly the flat road that crosses the plain from Dachau to the suburbs of Munich is lit up by the electric headlights of fast police cars.

'*Schuppos!*' shout the Storm Troopers. Police!

A police lieutenant orders Strasser's convoy to stop.

'Where are you going?' Gregor Strasser asks the commanding police officer.

'Same as you – Munich.'

'Are you with us or against us?'

'I don't know yet. We shall receive our orders upon arrival in Munich.' The commanding police lieutenant is Georg Höfler. He is Gregor Strasser's brother-in-law.

'Good luck!' They shake hands.

The 3,000 Storm Troopers reach the Munich parade ground of Oberwiesenfeld. All Hitler's bodyguard troops are there, as well as the Storm Troopers under Hermann Göring, one of the nation's great war heroes and holder of the highest war decoration in Germany. Göring has returned from self-imposed exile in Sweden after the last war and is married to an elegant and wealthy Swedish woman. The former commander of the famous Richthofen Air Squadron is wearing his old war uniform that has grown too tight for him. Adolf Hitler is dressed in a self-made uniform with a heavy steel helmet. Captain Röhm wants to speak to Hitler.

'What is happening?' Hitler asks.

'The time is not ripe yet,' says Captain Röhm. 'North Germany is not ready. General Ludendorff is forbidden to enter or remain in Munich.'

The Storm Troopers return to Landshut.

But Hitler wants action, and action is what he'll get. Somewhere near Munich, Captain Röhm has stored a secret cache of surplus war material.

Moeller van den Bruck intends to travel to Italy and visit the Monte Verità commune in Ascona where writers, sun-worshippers, anthroposophists, artists and philosophers gather in search of an alternative way of life that is close to nature. But soon after the publication of *The Third Reich* on 24 August 1923, Moeller van den Bruck starts hallucinating. He distrusts everyone, even those close to him. He suspects everyone of spying on him. His anxieties become unbearable. He suffers from nightmares and insomnia, and takes sleeping-pills as well as sleeping-powders. Since he suffers from various neurotical complaints, he is prescribed pervatin, Dexedrene, caffeine, cocaine and netraseptyl as well as Dr Koestner's anti-gas pills which contain strychnine and astrophene.

His mental condition is deteriorating. He lives in virtual seclusion. At night, he wanders around restlessly; the sleeping-powder does not help. Sometimes he awakes from a short sleep in crying fits. His nightmares increase in frequency and intensity, and drive him closer to nervous collapse. For hours he sits in an armchair, shivering, covered with blankets. If he sleeps at night he often wakes up shouting for help, and sits on the edge of his bed unable to move, shaking with fear. The whole bed vibrates. He yells out confused, unintelligible phrases. He gasps, as if imagining himself to be suffocating. On more than one occasion he stands swaying in his room, looking wildly about him. 'He's been here!' he gasps. His lips are blue. Sweat streams down his face. He begins to reel off names and figures, odd words, broken phrases. He uses strangely composed and entirely un-German word formations. Then he stands still, only his lips moving. Suddenly he breaks out again. 'There! There! In the corner! Who's that?' he stamps and shrieks. There is no one there.

Doctors who examine Moeller van den Bruck report degenerative brain damage to the lower brain centres caused by nervous syphilitic attacks. They advise treatment in a specialized asylum.

Where did Moeller van den Bruck get his ideas from, and who are the precursors who influenced his formation of *The Third Reich*? First and foremost, there is Nietzsche. His demonic figure looms large over Moeller van den Bruck's magnum opus. *Power* is the keynote to all of Nietzsche's writings. Power and megalomania. In Nietzsche's autobiography, chapters are entitled 'Why I am so Wise' and 'Why I am so Clever'. In *The Will to Power* Nietzsche bluntly states: 'Society has never regarded virtue as anything else than as a means to power and order. The State is the will to war, to power, to conquest and revenge.'

Nietzsche is convinced that the future of German culture rests on the shoulders of the sons of Prussian officers. In a pure nineteenth-century spirit, Nietzsche describes the coming *Ubermensch* or 'superman' – a term he borrowed from Goethe's *Faust* – as a new, biologically more valuable, racially improved, stronger type of man, with a greater capacity for survival and preservation of the species than all who lived before him. Nietzsche's 'superman', perfect in body and mind and who delights in battle, is happy in the consciousness of his own strength, and disdains man-made laws and man-made gods. What is soft must become hard; man must become superman, trained for war. Those who are weak and sick must be eliminated for the superman will not weaken himself by feeling pity. 'There is no such thing as a right to live, the right to work, or the right to be happy,' writes Nietzsche. 'In this respect, man is no different from the meanest worm. Society can only be a scaffolding for a select race of supermen to elevate themselves to higher duties.' The complete man is the complete beast. Nietzsche longs to see the strong, hard, barbarian Teutonic Knights of former times revived in a new aristocracy of *Ubermenschen.*

In *Thus spoke Zarathustra*, the most famous of his books, he writes: 'You shall love peace only as a means to war, and the short peace more than the long peace. Do not work, but fight. War and courage have done more great things than charity.' Nietzsche is, of course, opposed to parliamentary democracy and to a free press, 'because they create the possibility for cattle to become masters'.

Nietzsche's active career as a writer spans almost exactly the age of Bismarck. His first major publication,

The Birth of Tragedy, was begun during the Franco-Prussian war and the last work to be completed prior to his final breakdown, *The Twilight of the Idols*, appeared in the year before Bismarck's dismissal, in 1889. It is fair to say that the ghost of Nietzsche overlaps the Second Reich. From 1890 on, Nietzsche became widely known and talked about, as 'the fashionable philosopher' and 'the event of the time'.

Second only to Nietzsche in Moeller van den Bruck's panoply of precursors, there is the undeniable influence of composer Richard Wagner on the creation of *The Third Reich*. Wagner's popular success in bringing about a romantic German ideal in hedonistic operas such as *Tristan und Isolde*, *Lohengrin*, *The Flying Dutchman* and *Götterdammerung* coincided with the triumph of Bismarck's Second Reich. It was a time when grand show-piece buildings are erected: the 2.2-mile long Kürfurstendamm in Berlin, the Maximilian-Strasse in Munich, the Ring in Vienna, all lined with splendid works of architecture. The emperor had proclaimed that any 'art' which ventured beyond the laws and limits imposed by himself was no longer 'art'. Wagner was profoundly convinced that it was his destiny to compose works that would give expression to the true Germany. Not only in his music, but also in a stream of books and pamphlets, he attacked prevailing conventions and defended his pessimistic philosophy, which was strongly influenced by Schopenhauer. In the 1870s, so-called 'Wagner Societies' sprang up throughout Germany. A wave of triumphant nationalism and 'beer-mug patriotism' carried Wagner's operas to the height of their popularity.

Personally linked to Wagner through marriage is

English writer Houston Stewart Chamberlain who has been called 'one of the strangest Englishmen who ever lived'. Born at Southsea in 1855, the son of an admiral and nephew of a field marshal – Sir Neville Chamberlain – and two generals, Houston Stewart Chamberlain was clearly intended for the British army. But ill health made a military career impossible, and Chamberlain turned to his school books. He studied botany, geology, astronomy and medical sciences in Versailles, Geneva and at Cheltenham College; in Dresden he plunged into the study of Wagner's writings and his music. For almost a decade Houston Stewart Chamberlain lived in Vienna; then he took on German nationality. He was a highly neurotic man, one would have said slightly mad, but since he belonged to the upper classes, he was instead labelled 'eccentric'. He could write fluently in French and German as well as English.

In 1899, on the eve of the twentieth century, Houston Stewart Chamberlain produced his best known book in German, *Foundations of the Nineteenth Century*, in which he regards the Teutonic Knights not as barbarians and destroyers but as saviours and survivors. The book is animated by an aristocratic scorn of the masses and a romantic conception of the Germans as a master race with a mission to rule the world. For Chamberlain, race is the most important factor in historical development. Men must be judged like dogs and racehorses, writes Houston Stewart Chamberlain: 'The man who belongs to a pure race never loses the sense of it.' Although he praises Judaism for its 'racial purity', he also considers the Jew an alien in German society: 'To this day, Jews and Teutons stand face to face.' Race lifts a man above himself; it endows him with almost superhuman power.

The Teutonic invaders are superheroes with great radiant heavenly eyes, golden hair, gigantic stature, lengthened skull and an ever-active brain. 'Teutonic Europe' is 'the beating heart and thinking brain of all mankind'. In his country of origin, Houston Stewart Chamberlain's *Foundations of the Nineteenth Century* had no following whatsoever, but in Germany the book became a great success. Three editions were sold in three years, and by 1909 it had gone through eight editions.

Before his abdication, Kaiser Wilhelm II publicly admitted the strong influence Chamberlain's writings had upon him. They exchanged enthusiastic letters on the subject of Germany, and praised each other repeatedly. 'Your Majesty and your subjects have been born in a holy shrine,' Chamberlain wrote to the emperor, to which Wilhelm II replied: 'I invoke God's blessing upon my comrade and ally in the fight for Germans against Rome and Jerusalem.'

At an advanced age, Houston Stewart Chamberlain divorced his mentally unstable and physically ill Prussian wife and married Eva, Richard Wagner's daughter.

Another precursor of fame who covers the same ground as Houston Stewart Chamberlain is the romantic poet Stefan George (1868–1933), who was deeply impressed by Nietzsche's image of the 'superman'. With Hermann Hesse, Stefan George is the most important literary figure of the pre-war period. He lived in Paris for a while, participated in the symbolist soirées of Mallarmé and was strongly influenced by Baudelaire, Verlaine and Dante, whose works he translated into German. Himself a writer of sombre, measured, melodious and powerful poetry in which words such as Reich and Führer figure prominently, Stefan George believes in the vision of the poet, in aristocracy of the spirit, and in the revival of the Teutonic supremacy. He is attracted by the idea of ruthless, unlimited power and predicts the birth of a hero who will plant the seeds of a new Reich and lead first of all Germany, then 'a European Union', and finally 'the world government' into a new 'World Order'. In dramatic fashion, Stefan George advocates a secret academy called 'the George Circle', with himself as the high priest and Nietzsche as one of its apostles. Wearing only black clothes of a clerical cut and using the swastika as his symbol, he moves from city to city preaching to a small audience of devoted followers the benefits of a Reich that is an idealized Utopia, and therefore not of this world.

Apart from Nietzsche, Wagner, Chamberlain and Stefan George, Martin Luther is the fifth German 'philosopher' who is Moeller van den Bruck's main inspiration leading him to his concept and completion of *The Third Reich*. Moeller van den Bruck is a descendant not only of a family of architects but also of evangelical pastors. To this day, a portrait painting of the deacon Johann Melchior Moeller (1694–1761), one of his oldest known ancestors, is prominently displayed in the Kaufmannskirche (the Traders' Church) in Erfurt.

From his childhood days, Moeller van den Bruck is instilled with the teachings of the man who launches the German Reformation and has aroused through his sermons and his own Bible translation a new Protestant vision of Christianity. Martin Luther (1483–1546) is a coarse, intolerant, savage anti-Semite; originally a peasant, he becomes an Augustinian monk. It is Luther's idea that men's dual nature – the physical and the spiritual – calls for two 'governments', one secular and one spiritual. This concept of two 'governments' separates private from public morality. Lutheran pastors have preached for generations that the good Christian should be loving, forgiving, kind and honest in his personal life, whereas the nation may be ruthless, cruel, harsh, deceitful, calculating and machiavellian. For Luther, there is no doubt that God has chosen the German people to perform a special mission in history and that good Christians owe absolute obedience to the German nation because its rulers, right or wrong, are agents of God.

Hitler incessantly drums up support. Money comes in mainly from collections at the mass meetings at which Hitler makes speeches about war and fighting, and from outside donations. The party's principal financiers are the chairman of the Bavarian Federation of Industrialists and his son-in-law, who have the dual functions of being founder of Bayerischen Motoren Werke (BMW) and president of the Deutsche Bank. From abroad, financial aid is received from Switzerland, Holland and Czechoslovakia where directors of the French-controlled Skoda armaments works are a pillar of financial support to the Hitler cause. American car manufacturer Henry Ford is approached by Nazi agents from Germany with a request for a contribution. Sir Henry Deterding, head of the Shell Oil concern and owner of Russian oil wells confiscated by the Bolsheviks, takes a financial interest in Hitler.

The back room in the Sterneckerbräu is given up and new rooms, lighter and roomier, are found in another beer hall in the Cornelius-Strasse. They look more like an office, with a safe, filing cabinets, a telephone and a full-time secretary. An Adler typewriter is purchased. The party has acquired a rundown, anti-Semitic Munich gossip tabloid which appears twice a week, the *Völkische Beobachter* (People's Observer). The 60,000 marks for its acquisition have been advanced by the Bechstein family. When the *Völkische Beobachter* becomes a daily, party philosopher Alfred Rosenberg becomes its first editor. Hitler uses the newsroom as a conference room to hold his political reunions.

Privately, Hitler lives in a modest two-room flat in the Thier-Strasse 41, in a lower middle-class district near the River Isar. The floor of the flat is covered with linoleum and cheap rugs. His only books are popular history books and Clausewitz's *On War* which he can quote at length. Above his bed hangs a portrait of his mother. In the mornings, Hitler is always whistling to himself or humming a tune. He wears an old trench coat in winter and traditional Bavarian Lederhosen (leather shorts) in summer. Sometimes he likes to show off, wearing a leather aviator's helmet. He enjoys target shooting and enthusiastically takes part in pistol practice.

Hitler has forbidden anyone in his immediate circle to wear a moustache or a beard. The only exemption on the moustache edict is Julius Schreck who is his driver and bodyguard. Schreck is nicknamed 'Pistol Schreck' because he carries a revolver in every pocket that can hold one. He is a primitive, brutal, animal-type of a man, utterly devoted to Hitler. One day, he contracts an abscessed tooth. He takes a screwdriver from his tool case, gouges and scrapes the infected tooth, brakes up the abscess, and amid horrible pain pulls out the tooth with a pair of pliers. Mad with pain and fever, Schreck is taken to the hospital, where he dies. Ulrich Graf, a butcher and a wrestler, takes over as personal bodyguard to Hitler.

In order to bring the Weimar Republic down, Hitler plans a march on Berlin, in imitation of Mussolini's march on Rome. Hitler admires Mussolini more than any other foreign politician.

Part of the summer of 1923 Hitler spends in Berlin. He brings Helene Bechstein an extraordinary bouquet of roses, which he presents to his hostess. He gallantly kisses her hand. Hitler is dressed in a decent blue suit. He thanks the lady of the house for tea and cakes and eats an amazing quantity of them.

Helene Bechstein presents Hitler with a signed copy of *The Third Reich* by Moeller van den Bruck. In a harsh, emotional and penetrating voice, Hitler comments on the book. In the next room, a child wakes up and begins to cry.

Later that week, Hitler and the Bechstein family visit 'Wahnfried', the home of the Wagner family in Bayreuth. Hitler is dressed in Bavarian leather breeches, thick woollen socks, a red and blue check shirt and a short blue jacket. The Nazi Party leader captivates Houston Stewart Chamberlain, the aged and almost blind philosopher of nineteenth-century civilization. The dying Briton who adopted German nationality murmurs: '. . . *Heil!*

Hitler jumps up, clicks his heels together, and takes his leave. He then visits the grand and impressive Nietzsche-Archiv and Library in Weimar.

A middle-aged Nobel Prize-winning German professor named Albert Einstein thinks he is growing senile because he hasn't made any progress in general relativity or in the unified field theory. 'A softening of the brain,' he calls it. He tries literature as a stimulant and reads Dostoyevsky's *The Brothers Karamazov* in German translation. It is the best book he has ever read. To a fellow professor at Berlin University, he confides: 'No one knows in what direction the political ship is drifting. The Weimar Republic has sunk to its lowest ebb of impotence.' A Berliner is offering a reward to anyone who kills the most famous Jew in Germany. The police informs Albert Einstein that he is on a death list of a group planning to assassinate influential Jews. Other targets on the death list are Theodor Wolff, the editor of the *Berliner Tageblatt*, and Max Warburg, a banker.

The Weimar Republic is in deep trouble. Matthias Erzberger has been murdered. He had the courage to sign the armistice when the generals backed out. There has been an attempt to assassinate Scheidemann who proclaimed the Weimar Republic from the open window in the Reichstag building. Foreign Minister Walther Rathenau is riddled with machine-gun bullets by hired killers. He tried to work out some of the provisions of the Versailles Treaty.

In one of his speeches, Adolf Hitler says that the two young men who killed Rathenau are 'German heroes'. The murder of Rathenau is timed to coincide with the summer solstice; he has been offered up as a human sacrifice to the sun-god of ancient Germanic mythology. Kurt Eisner, a popular Jewish writer and prime minister of the short-lived Bavarian People's Republic, is assassinated. In all three cases, the political murder is plotted in Munich. Berlin demands an end to political gangsterism and orders the suppression of Hitler's *Völkische Beobachter* because of its hateful attacks on the Weimar Republic and its leaders. At a party rally in Nuremberg, Hitler appears next to Ludendorff. Storm Troopers in their extravagant brown shirts with multicoloured flags and swastika armbands hail for a Hitler–Ludendorff dictatorship.

Hitler sits with Hess and a few others in the editorial office above the printing plant of the *Völkische Beobachter* in Schelling-Strasse. Editor-in-chief Alfred Rosenberg comes in with the news that the following evening the State Commissioner is to speak in the Bürgerbrau, a large beer hall in the Rosenheimer-Strasse on the outskirts of the city. The local Reichswehr commander and the Bavarian head of the State Police will be present.

'The State Commissioner will proclaim Bavaria's independence and reinstall the monarchy!' Hess hisses excitedly.

'This is our chance!' Hitler smiles.

'What will we do?' asks Hess.

Hitler looks at Hess briefly. 'Join your men and wait for orders.'

Hess is dismissed. He commands 600 Storm Troopers who have been drilled military-style in the woods outside Munich. Alfred Rosenberg draws up a text for the posters proclaiming the national revolution. Then he plans the layout for the *Völkische Beobachter* front page dated 8 November 1923.

The dollar stands at 4,200,000,000 marks.

The borders of Bavaria are closed. The Reichswehr moves into position. The break with Berlin seems complete. Nazi Party membership has risen to 50,000.

At the entrance of the Bürgerbrau beer hall, Hitler keeps asking to speak to the State Commissioner. He is pale and trembling, and looks like a madman. Inside the beer hall, the meeting has already begun. Hitler hesitates, but it is too late to turn back.

'Clear the vestibule!' he orders a policeman on duty at the entrance. The policeman obeys.

A few minutes later, Hitler's Storm Troopers march in. Hitler waits for them with his eyes closed, his hands in his pockets. He is dressed in his best suit with a long frock coat on which he has pinned his Iron Cross. A machine-gun is mounted in the entrance, the muzzle pointed at the front door of the beer hall.

Then Hitler enters the Bürgerbrau; 3,000 thirsty Bavarians are seated at rough wooden tables drinking beer out of stone mugs, Bavarian-style. Hitler pushes forward into the hall and jumps onto a table. It is 8.30 p.m. He fires a revolver shot toward the ceiling.

'The national revolution has begun!' Hitler shouts. 'The Bürgerbrau is surrounded by heavily armed men. No one may leave the hall. The barracks of Reichswehr and police have been taken over. From this moment on, police and the army are marching under the swastika banner!' Hitler is bluffing, but no one knows if he is speaking the truth or not. Hitler's revolver is real. The Storm Troopers in their brown shirts are real. Their rifles from Captain Röhm's secret cache are real. The machine-gun at the entrance is real.

The State Commissioner who is speaking falls silent in astonishment. Hitler calls on the policemen on duty to surrender. Beer mugs start flying like howitzers above Hitler's head. Someone shouts to the police: 'Don't be cowards as you were in 1918. Shoot!' At the point of his revolver, Hitler commands the State Commissioner, the local Reichswehr commander and the head of the State Police into an adjourning back room.

Göring steps on the rostrum. 'There is nothing to fear,' he says in a quiet voice. 'We have the most friendly intentions. Don't make a fuss, drink your beer.'

In the back room, a new government is being formed. Hitler informs his prisoners that they will be given key jobs in his Reich government. The State Commissioner will become the Regent of Bavaria, the Reichswehr commander minister of the National Army and the head of the local police minister of the Reich Police.

'To whom will you entrust the political control of Germany?' ask the three men.

Hitler answers simply: 'Myself! I propose to assume the political leadership of the National Government until we have dealt with the criminals who are bringing our country to ruin.'

Ludendorff has arrived. People start chanting when the general, known to everyone, appears on the platform. He is deadly pale, as events have taken him by surprise. But he does not lose his composure. He turns to the crowd and tells them that victory is theirs. 'At my own authority, I declare that I put myself at the disposal of the National Government,' he announces.

Hitler, meanwhile, waves his gun at his three prisoners. 'I have four shots in my revolver! Three for you, and the last bullet is for myself. If I am not victorious by tomorrow afternoon, we shall all be dead!'

'Dying or not dying is not important,' the State Commissioner answers.

The local head of the State Police blames Hitler for breaking his word of honour never to make a putsch against the police. 'Forgive me,' Hitler replies, 'but I had to, for the sake of our Fatherland.' He dashes back into the beer hall. 'A new national government will be named this very evening here in Munich!' he shouts. 'General Ludendorff will take over the leadership of the German National Army. We will organize a march on that sinful Babel – Berlin! – and save the German people!' Three thousand Bavarians drunk with joy and beer leap onto the benches and the tables in a delirium of enthusiasm.

'This is an event in world history!' exclaims General Ludendorff.

Hitler speaks his final words: 'I will honour the oath I swore to myself five years ago when I was a blind cripple in the military hospital. I will know neither rest nor peace until the criminals of the Weimar Republic have been overthrown, and until on the ruins of the wretched Germany of today there will arise a Germany of power and greatness!'

The meeting breaks up. Gregor Strasser marches his ex-soldiers to Munich's main railway station, singing patriotic songs. They catch a late evening train back to Landshut, and return home. Hess and Captain Röhm remain at the Bürgerbrau at the head of their Storm Troopers. They make their quarters for the night on the floor of the beer hall and in the gardens.

Shortly before noon the next day, Hitler begins to suspect treachery. The time passes, with no news from his three prisoners. Hitler and General Ludendorff lead almost 3,000 storm troopers out of the gardens of the Bürgerbrau beer hall. It is 9 November 1923, the fourth anniversary of the proclamation of the Weimar Republic. Hitler has decided on a 'propaganda march' through the city. They head for the centre of Munich. Hess hoists up the swastika flag on the roof of the city hall. Defences with barbed wire and machine-guns are set up. Munich is full of soldiers and police. There are swastikas everywhere. A makeshift truck loaded with machine-guns and war veteran sharpshooters follow the parade. The Storm Troopers have carbines with fixed bayonets slung over their shoulders. Behind the first ranks drives another motor lorry with machine-guns ready to fire. Hitler and Ludendorff march side by side. Hitler carries his revolver.

On the Ludwig Bridge which leads over the River Isar towards the city centre, a detachment of armed police bars the road. Göring thrusts himself forward and threatens to shoot a number of hostages including two government members held prisoner in the rear of the column. They file over the bridge unmolested. At the Marienplatz the Storm Troopers encounter a large crowd listening to Julius Streicher from Nuremberg. He has rushed to Munich on the first news of the putsch. Streicher cuts short his speech and jumps into step immediately behind Hitler. The brownshirts file through the narrow Residenz-Strasse which opens into the spacious Odeonsplatz just beyond the Feldherrnhalle (Hall of Heroes). A police detachment with machine-guns blocks the way.

Hitler's bodyguard cries out to the police officer in charge: 'Do not shoot! General Ludendorff is commanding!'

'Surrender!' shouts Hitler. He fires the first shot. Then Streicher starts shooting. A volley of shots rings out from both sides. Pandemonium follows. The first to be fatally wounded is Erich von Scheibner-Richter. Göring gets a bullet in his leg, and is badly injured in the groin. Others are lying around, dead or wounded, bleeding heavily. Within less than a minute, the street is littered with 16 dead bodies.

General Ludendorff, erect and proud in the best soldierly tradition, marches calmly through the narrow Residenz-Strasse towards the whizzing bullets until he reaches the Odeonsplatz and the Feldherrnhalle. Then the policemen turn their guns away from the great war hero.

Hitler picks himself up from the pavement and runs back to the bottom of the Residenz-Strasse. He has dislocated his shoulder. A yellow motor car suddenly drives into the crowd. Emil Maurice shouts: 'Where is Hitler?'

'Here he is!' answers a Storm Trooper. Moments later the car drives Hitler out of Munich.

General Ludendorff is arrested on the spot. Göring is given first aid by the Jewish proprietor of a nearby bank into which he has been carried. Then he flees to Innsbruck, from where he travels on to Italy and then to Sweden. There he enters a nursing home and undergoes a cure for morphine addiction. Hess is being driven south, in the direction of Bad-Tölz. He takes a mountain path familiar to him from his frequent hikes there with his girlfriend, and escapes into Austria. Captain Röhm surrenders to the police in front of the Feldherrnhalle. Two days later, Hitler is arrested at the house of his publisher friend Putzi Hanfstäengl. In his hide-out in Austria, Hess buys a local newspaper. He reads: 'Adolf Hitler arrested in wardrobe of a villa on the Staffel-Lake.' Two hundred and sixteen Nazi prisoners are taken into custody in connection with the beer hall putsch.

Gregor Strasser and his deputy Heinrich Himmler sit down for lunch in Landshut when his brother-in-law

Georg Höfler enters the pharmacy. 'You're just in time,' Gregor Strasser says. 'Why don't you join us for lunch?'

'I've come to arrest you,' Georg Höfler answers formally. Escorted by his brother-in-law, Gregor Strasser is locked up in Landshut prison.

On 26 February 1924 the trial of Adolf Hitler and General Ludendorff begins before a special court sitting in the building of the former Infantry School. They are accused of having attempted to overthrow by violence the Bavarian government and the Weimar Republic. Correspondents of all the leading German newspapers, as well as of the world press, have come to Munich to cover the trial.

The prisoners stand in the dock. Hitler immediately grabs the limelight. Stepping before the judge, he bows respectfully to the president of the court and declares: 'Yes, I wanted to destroy the Weimar Republic! I alone am responsible. But I am not a criminal. And I did not plan a revolution. On the contrary, I wish to help the government in creating the unity of our country. I am a revolutionary against the revolution. I want to become the destroyer of Marxism, and I am going to achieve this task. I am born to be a dictator!' He needs four hours for his opening statement.

Hitler is allowed to interrupt the judiciary as often as he pleases, to cross-examine witnesses at will and to speak on his own behalf at any time and at any length. The judges carefully avoid asking awkward questions. Hitler testifies that he has left Vienna as an absolute anti-Semite and a sworn enemy of the whole Marxist world outlook. He refers to Bismarck, Mustafa Kemal Ataturk and Mussolini – 'the great man beyond the

Alps' – as men who have acted arbitrarily and against the constitution, but whose actions have been justified by their results. In the course of his peroration, he speaks of General Ludendorff. At such moments, he stands at attention. In his closing address, Hitler plays on the idea of reconciliation with the armed forces: 'I believe that the hour will come when the Reichswehr will unite under our swastika banner.'

The president of the court refers to Hitler's military decorations and to his bravery in the field during the war. Hitler smells valuable publicity. He gives an idealized account of his career, and of his aims. Hitler speaks his final words: 'You may pronounce us guilty a thousand times over, but history will smile and tear to tatters the sentence of this court.'

The audience in the courtroom is spellbound. General Ludendorff is acquitted. Captain Röhm is released on probation. Whatever the outcome of his trial, Hitler has turned it into a triumphant propaganda presentation. He has become the political hero of the conservative right overnight. Police efforts to get Hitler deported as a foreigner – since he still is an Austrian citizen – come to nothing. For high treason and attempted armed putsch, Hitler is sentenced to five years' imprisonment in the fortress of Landsberg. The presiding judge assures that the prisoner will be eligible for parole after he has served six months, one-tenth of his sentence. Rudolf Hess returns to Munich and turns himself in to the authorities. He is sentenced to 18 months' imprisonment. Hitler has catapulted his hardly known Nazi Party into the headlines throughout Germany and the world.

As a result of the trial in Munich, Moeller van den Bruck comments in the weekly *The Conscience* to which he is the principal editorialist: 'There are many things that can be said against Hitler, and I have sometimes said them. But one thing you have to give him credit for: he is a fanatic for Germany. But he is wrecked by his proletarian primitive ways. He does not know how to give an intellectual basis to his Nazi Party. Hitler is all passion, but lacks sense or proportion. A heroic tenor, not a hero.' They will be his last words in print. His message is clear – Moeller van den Bruck does not see in Hitler a man of the stature of Mussolini.

Then he collapses, and sinks into total lethargy; a state of gloom, of utter darkness, of suicidal despondency. His dreams are troubled and he wakes up, struggling with himself, and cries aloud: 'I will sleep no more!'

Franz Kafka comes from Prague to Berlin with the idea of settling there. With Dora Dymant (Diamant), his fiancée, he moves into furnished rooms in the Miquel-Strasse in Berlin-Steglitz, a side street around the corner from where Moeller van den Bruck lives. They have two rooms with a veranda. Kafka begins to see Berlin as a stepping stone to Palestine. He observes his neighbourhood and writes: 'My road is the last one that is more or less urban; then everything dissolves peacefully into gardens and villas.'

During his first month in Berlin, Franz Kafka and Dora eat in a restaurant only once. Inflation makes restaurants and theatre tickets too expensive. He writes a short story, *Eine kleine Frau* (A little woman) in which he portrays his sour landlady, who is not pleased with the presence of Dora in the house. For relaxation, he walks

in the nearby botanical gardens. Kafka writes: 'I find
the city centre frightful.' In order to prepare himself for
emigration to Palestine, he studies the Old Testament
with the commentary in Hebrew. He works through
the night, with the use of a paraffin lamp because
the landlady is upset about the electricity he consumes.
Kafka is given notice at the end of his sixth week in
the house.

He and Dora move to two rooms in the Grünewald-
Strasse 13 in the villa of a female doctor, Dr Rethburg,
opposite the botanical gardens and the evangelical
church. On his daily walk, Franz Kafka sees a little girl
who is crying because she has lost her doll. He explains
to the girl that the doll is away, travelling, but surely
will write to her. For weeks afterwards, Kafka sends
the girl letters in which the doll describes her travel
adventures. His living conditions have never been
worse. Since he cannot pay for the gas stove, he cooks
his food on two methylated spirit burners and an oven
improvised out of a tin. When they cannot afford to
buy spirit any longer, Dora uses candles to heat their
food. The rent has become too much, and again they
have to move. They find a single room in Zehlendorf,
not far from the Grünewald, in what Kafka describes
as a *überschönes* (wonderful) house. It belongs to the
widow of the novelist Dr Carl Busse, who died in 1918.

Seriously ill, Kafka doesn't have the money to enter
a sanatorium, and he cannot afford a second-class bed
in the Jewish Hospital either. He coughs mornings and
evenings; at the end of each day, his sputum bottle is
full. Kafka insists that Dora burns his manuscripts. On
17 March 1924, Kafka returns to Prague. Three months
later, he is dead.

At first, the aborted putsch has a devastating impact on the National Socialist movement. The party is banned in Prussia and Bavaria. The offices of the *Völkische Beobachter* are shut down. From the remnants of the Nazi Party, General Ludendorff sets up the rival National Socialist Freedom Party. He is the party figurehead, but he lacks the drive and stamina for successful political leadership. In the Bavarian elections of 1924, the 'new' Nazi Party gains 27 seats. The Nazi vote numbers nearly 2 million.

Gregor Strasser is elected Member of Parliament. He is permitted to leave the fortress prison of Landshut without serving the remainder of his term. Gregor Strasser takes on the party leadership, acting as deputy for Adolf Hitler. He is a genuine Bavarian: large, balding, powerfully built, dressed in home-made breeches, black woollen stockings and heavy shoes, with a little Tyrolean hat perched like a plate on top of his head. Gregor Strasser is roughly the same age as Hitler. In his speeches, he calls democracy a mask concealing the domination of capitalist businesses. The idea that economic interests take precedence over ideas of honour and Fatherland is utter nonsense. Marxism is a destructive doctrine, anti-German and anti-cultural. Jewish agitators lead a power struggle of international high finance.

The serious wounds Gregor Strasser suffered in the war continue to trouble him in his political career. The only people he trusts and respects are the war veterans who still have the courage to challenge the liberal government. Strasser is not only party leader in Munich, he also holds a parliamentary mandate in Berlin. He is determined to put his free railway pass to good use, and actively starts organizing the Nazi Party in the north of Germany.

Hitler decides to retire from politics until his release from Landsberg prison.

Instead of a weekly journal, the new Nazi publication in Berlin will not be a magazine but an evening paper, the *Berliner Arbeiterzeitung* (Berlin Worker's Paper). Its editor is Otto Strasser, while his brother Gregor takes on the mantle of publisher. They also circulate a fortnightly newsletter intended for party officials to keep them informed of the party line. Joseph Goebbels becomes secretary to Gregor Strasser and editor of the party newsletter. He writes in his diary: 'Publisher: Strasser. Editor – *moi!* Just as we want it.' He exclaims, 'Heil! Heil!!', and draws a swastika. But the salary is inadequate to make ends meet. He complains that his debts are weighing on him. He prepares the first issue of the party newsletter, and writes in his diary: 'Had a long and fruitful talk with Gregor Strasser. Complete unanimity is reached. Strasser isn't nearly as much of a bourgeois as I took him to be. I want Strasser to be my friend.' Goebbels notes that he is 'deeply impressed' by General Ludendorff who has spoken to him 'for a long time'.

He is asked to draft a new party programme, and confides to his diary that the Strasser brothers have turned to him in despair. Meanwhile, he gains experience as a speaker and an agitator. He rehearses like an actor, and is more concerned with the effect he has on his audience than with the significance of what he is saying. At the end of a meeting, he records: 'I preached for two hours. A breathless, spellbound audience. 1,000 beer mugs broken, 150 Communists wounded, two dead.' Goebbels is interrogated by the police who want to bring charges for causing riots. 'In so many German towns,' he writes, 'blood is flowing for our ideas. Munich and Berlin are burning! I want to be an apostle and a preacher.' Almost daily, Goebbels commits his thoughts and experiences to paper, often at formidable length. 'Can you beat the Jews in any other way than with their own weapons?' he asks. Then he writes: 'Nothing but reproaches from Hitler himself! . . . Bloody fools in Munich.'

FIVE

The Asylum

In a wooded valley in the small romantic town of Landsberg-on-the-Lech, a good hour's drive south-west of Munich, is sited a modern, clean building in a large orchard. It looks like a sanatorium; in fact, it is a penal institution with all up-to-date conveniences. Adolf Hitler lives on the first floor, in a spacious two-windowed sunny room, with an open view of the countryside. The inhabitants on the first floor are regarded as the privileged 'upper class'. Besides Hitler and Hess, only Emil Maurice and Christian Weber live on the first floor. Weber is well known to the Munich police as a 'protector' of local prostitutes. Emil Maurice serves Hitler as a cleaner. Both are allowed to call Hitler 'Adi'. The other prisoners in Landsberg live on the ground floor in small cells. Among them is Walther Meyer, Hitler's manservant. The men on the ground floor are playing knuckle-bones and other games as a pastime.

Hitler's prison furniture consists of a bed, a wicker chair, a wardrobe and a large working table. Behind his wicker chair on the wall is a gilded laurel wreath given to him by his admirers. Also in his room hangs a Dürer woodcut, *Death and the Knight*, dating from 1510, and a portrait of his mother. Hitler is always immaculately dressed in tie and collar, as worn in the city. When he takes a walk in the afternoon, he changes to leather shorts with a Tyrolean jacket. Occasionally he does some gardening. The prisoners on the ground floor have to rise at 6 a.m. and turn the lights off at 10 p.m. Hitler is allowed to sleep as long as he likes. Each morning he takes some exercise for 20 minutes, naked. Walther Meyer counts for him: '*Eins . . . zwei . . .*' Meyer suggests that Hitler should box with him. They spar with bare fists. Hitler recounts that while a pupil at the Realschule in Linz, he had excellent marks only in gymnastics. In the evenings, he turns off the light whenever he likes. He is permitted to read or work until midnight or longer. Hitler's door is always open, and Hess and Emil Maurice can visit him whenever they want. Lunch and dinner are taken in the communal dining-room.

One day Hitler asks at the lunch table: 'Have you read Trotsky's book?' Hess answers: 'Yes, a revolting book! The memoirs of Satan!' To which Hitler replies: 'Revolting? Brilliant, I should say. What a brain! Trotsky's book has taught me a great deal.'

Hitler is showered with so many letters and gifts that he ends up dividing them among the guards. He receives a letter of encouragement from Houston Stewart Chamberlain, who writes: 'You have mighty things to do. My faith in Germany has not wavered an instant though my hope – I confess – was at a low ebb. With one stroke you have transformed the state of my soul. That Germany gives birth to Hitler in the hour of her deepest need proves her vitality. May God protect you.' On his thirty-fifth birthday, the parcels, letters and flowers Hitler is given fill several rooms. Hitler can order as many books and newspapers as he wishes. Helene Bechstein is generous in settling his bills. From Franz Thyssen, the powerful chairman of United Steelworks, he receives a gift of 100,000 gold marks.

Hitler uses his prison room as a private bedroom

only; he is allowed a second large room to work in, meet people and discuss politics. All the time, he receives lengthy visits from his political supporters. Helene Bechstein claims she is his adoptive mother so that she is allowed to visit him. They sit next to each other, with a guard who pretends to be asleep in a corner of the room. They talk politics and discuss daily topics. A Zeppelin has flown non-stop from Friedrichshafen in southern Germany to Lakehurst in New York in 81 hours and 17 minutes. When General Ludendorff and Gregor Strasser come to Landsberg for a visit, Hitler refuses to admit them. 'I do not surround myself with people having clever ideas of their own,' he says, 'but with people who are clever in finding ways to carry out *my* ideas.' Hitler abstains from identifying with any political party. He has no intention of conspiring against the legal government while he is in prison. 'It will take longer to defeat the Marxists in democratic elections than to shoot them,' he tells Hess, 'but in the end our success is guaranteed.' Hess asks Hitler how long it will take to assume power. 'At least five years,' Hitler answers, 'at most seven.'

In his first letter from Landsberg prison to his mother Klara in Reicholdsgrün, Rudolf Hess invokes a scene involving Hitler: 'I can hear his voice. He is with friends in the dining-room, recounting war memories. He imitates the sound of machine-guns and exploding grenades, and jumps up and down as if he is again in the trenches of Flanders.' On 8 May 1924: 'H[itler] does gymnastics! He doesn't smoke and only drinks some beer, no other alcohol. Today he designed our future Museum of the [First] World War. He intends to build a skyscraper as party headquarters. H[itler] said we should imitate America. Please don't send me another copy of Oswald Spengler's *The Decline of the West*. We've got at least four already. And H[itler] doesn't like the book.' To comply with censorship rules, Hess never mentions Hitler by name. He refers to Hitler as 'Herr H', 'H', 'the Master', 'the Tribune', 'the Dictator', 'the Chief' and 'the coming man'.

In a letter to Ilse Pohl, the girl from Berlin to whom he is engaged to be married, Hess mentions for the first time Hitler's book: 'At tea-time, H[itler] showed me the synopsis of a book he wants to write. He intends to publish two editions: a popular one as well as a parchment-bound deluxe edition. In a monotonous voice, H[itler] read to me the first draft of a trial chapter, about war propaganda.' The letter is dated 19 June 1924. Hess comes back to the theme of the book in a letter dated 10 July 1924: 'H[itler] intends to raise the question of women in politics in his book. Politics is men's business. H[itler] is of the opinion that, in politics, women should only be consulted on sanitary matters.' Two weeks later, in another letter to his fiancée: 'H[itler] came into my room and asked if I had time to listen to a chapter of his book he had just written, entitled 'Munich'. Such a lively, powerful and beautifully formulated chapter that blood rushed through my veins while I listened to H[itler]. *I love H[itler]!* When the book is published, a shock wave of anger and admiration will go through Germany.'

The very first sentence of Hitler's book reads more like the beginning of a fairy tale rather than a serious autobiography: 'Today it seems divine providence to me that fate chose Braunau-am-Inn as my birthplace.' Hitler is 35 years old. He tells the story of his life, and searches for the roots of his political philosophy. He also wants his book to be an accurate blueprint of what he intends to achieve in a future Nazi Germany. His primary theme is racial: the Germans should be a racially pure, superior Aryan people. Their destiny is world supremacy. Contaminated German blood has to be weeded out. It is the prime duty of the state to preserve and encourage its racial elements. The state is not an end, but a means to an end. Hitler describes the Weimar Republic as 'the greatest miscarriage of the Twentieth Century' and 'a monster of the human mechanism'. Germans are a chosen people upon whose survival the existence of man on this planet depends.

Thinking of his years in Vienna, Hitler laments: 'To me, Vienna represents five years of hardship and misery. It has been the saddest period of my life.' He admits to being influenced by great German thinkers and mentions Clausewitz, Schopenhauer and Houston Stewart Chamberlain. He also refers to Goethe, Schiller and even Shakespeare. Thirty-two pages are devoted to 'The World War' and nearly as much to syphilis, in an 'erotic' chapter that begins with some reflections on 'the scourge that is poisoning our sexual life' and in which he demands the sterilization of the incurably diseased. 'In large cities particularly,' writes Hitler, 'syphilis is reaping its harvest of death. The visible effect of this mass-infection can be observed in our insane asylums.'

Although the fate of Moeller van den Bruck is clearly on his mind, nowhere does Hitler mention his name and neither does he mention *The Third Reich* as the main source of inspiration for his own writings.

Page after page, Hitler acknowledges his belief in power, both will-power and physical force. 'The Second Reich,' Hitler writes, 'was born in dazzling splendour. The accompanying music was not the chatter of parliamentary debate, but the thunder and boom along the battle front.' He muses about new territory, German stock, the evils of the time, the Teutonic Knights, *Lebensraum*, the German plough and the German sword, and about ideas that can only be destroyed by even stronger ideas. In a phrasing worthy of Nietzsche in its cruel content, he unashamedly states that we live in a world where one creature feeds on another, a world in which the death of the weaker implies the life of the stronger.

In his last chapter, Hitler confesses that he entertains thoughts of exterminating Jews 'under poison gas'. He declares that he does not intend to address the masses with his book. 'With this work,' he makes clear, 'I do not address myself to strangers but to those disciples of the movement who seek more intimate information. I know that one is able to win people more by the spoken than by the written word, and that every great movement on this globe owes its rise to the great speakers and not to the great writers.' Hitler portrays himself as a man passionately and in an obsessed way in love with grandiose dreams, a man possessed, not unlike a character out of the pages of Dostoyevsky.

Karl Haushofer, a one-time general, is the spiritual father of the idea and political concept of *Lebensraum* or 'living space', a branch of study which he calls 'geopolitics'. Basically, he preaches a German world-space policy. His son Aelbrecht is one of the founding members of the June-Club in Berlin. The ex-general is Rudolf Hess's tutor at Munich University. Nearly every week he brings some reading to Hitler and Hess in Landsberg prison. Haushofer has lived in Japan and in the Middle East for several years. He pretends to understand the philosophy and the way of thinking of the 'yellow race'. For Haushofer, a league with] Japan is the alpha and omega of his 'geopolitics'. He stays in Landsberg for hours, discussing his ideas with Hess and Hitler. Hess takes notes.

Fellow prisoner Emil Maurice is furiously working on Hitler's manuscript on an adapted black portable Remington typewriter, the property of Emil Georg von Strauss, Deutsche Bank president and principal fund-raiser for the National Socialist Party. Emil Maurice is a passable stenographer and typist.

When Haushofer has gone, Hess sets himself at the typewriter while Hitler paces up and down the room, and dictates his wildest dreams. Hess does the editing on a number of chapters; he introduces new ideas and rearranges existing paragraphs. Hess and Emil Maurice make notes of every conversation with Hitler; they are the raw material for the final version of Hitler's book. While Hess is busy on the typewriter, Hitler makes architectural drawings, in which he decorates Munich with 'classical' party buildings, or he endlessly drums with his fingers on the table.

Even before the manuscript is complete, an agent of the publisher canvasses prospective buyers. On an advance payment of 5 marks for a copy of the book, the agent receives a commission of 3 marks. Sections of the manuscript are smuggled out of Landsberg prison by Helene Bechstein who visits Hitler on the pretext of bringing him phonograph records.

On 4 August 1924, barely four weeks after Hitler has showed him the synopsis and the first draft of a trial chapter, Rudolf Hess informs his fiancée Ilse Pohl that 'H[itler] hopes to finish his book sometime next week. We go through the text together.' Less than two weeks later, Hess writes a letter to his father, who is trying to recover the family business that has been expropriated in Alexandria, Egypt: 'Wake-up call. I make a cup of tea for H[itler], who has worked on his book throughout the night.' On 14 October 1924: 'Helene Bechstein has brought us a gramophone and some records: waltzes and military marches. A lovely voice sings Schubert and Wagner.'

Apart from Rudolf Hess, who takes most of the dictation, three men close to Hitler are involved with the writing and editing of the manuscript. First there is Emil Maurice, the only convict apart from Hitler and Hess who knows how to use a typewriter. Then there is Father Bernhard Staempfle, an anti-Semitic journalist and a former member of the Hieronymite order. He is the editor of a paper at Miessbach. Father Staempfle rewrites and edits Hitler's manuscript, corrects his grammar, works on his prose style and crosses out politically objectionable passages. He also eliminates the more flagrant inaccuracies. Twice Father Staempfle revises the whole manuscript. The third advisor is the poet Josef Czerny, of Czech origin, who worked as a reader on the *Völkische Beobachter*. He eliminates and changes embarrassing words and sentences, and cuts into the long, badly structured and repetitious, speech-like sentences. Hitler has a title in mind for his book: *Four and a Half Years of Struggle against Lies, Stupidity and Cowardice.*

On 20 December 1924, a telegram addressed to the commander of the fortress of Landsberg orders the immediate release of Adolf Hitler. The governor of Landsberg prison remarks in his final report on his behaviour: 'He is sober, modest, and obliging. He is not attracted to the female sex.' Hitler leaves the prison building that same day. Rudolf Hess's fiancée collects him in a rented car. They drive straight to Hitler's favourite restaurant, the Osteria Bavaria, the little Italian wine restaurant at the corner of Schelling-Strasse and Schraudolf-Strasse, across the street from the printing plant of the party newspaper and next door to Heinrich Hoffmann's photo studio. Hitler guzzles down a plate of ravioli, the speciality of the house. He is a politician without a party, but not for long.

Eleven days after Hitler, Hess too is released from prison. He immediately becomes Hitler's official private secretary on a monthly salary of 300 marks. At heart a soft and sensitive man, Hess is so devoted to Hitler that party members cheerfully call him 'Lady Hess'. Hess has his office installed in the house where Hoffmann keeps his photo studio. In the large mirror in Hoffmann's studio, Hitler rehearses the grandiose speeches he will one day give to the nation. He starts in a rather cautious manner, his tone of voice normal, and deals with his material in a fairly objective way. As he proceeds, his voice begins to rise, his tempo increases. His voice becomes louder and louder, the tempo faster and faster. Passion takes complete possession of him. Out of his mouth comes a veritable stream of curses, foul names, slander and hatred, a spasm of violence and cruelty. Like beats of a hammer, he works himself in a frenzy. When he suddenly stops, he is on the verge of exhaustion, his breathing heavy and uncontrolled. He is wet with perspiration. Pleased with himself, he says his shouting and gesturing are a spectacle people will pay to see.

The ban on the Nazi Party is lifted. The *Völkische Beobachter* is published on a daily basis. When Hitler is interviewed by *The Times* of London, he confidently declares that people will fall on their knees for a German Mussolini. He designs certificates for a promissory note, issued by the Nazi Party. The legend reads: 'Warrior of the Truth, Behead the Lie.' The Storm Troopers resume their activities. Hitler has his personal bodyguards wear the death's head as their insignia.

Together with Hess, he moves to the mountains south of Munich. Hitler whiles his time away in various inns in Berchtesgaden on the Obersalzberg, looking out across the towering ice-capped peaks of the Alps to his native Austria. First he lives in a boarding house, the Pension Moritz, then in the Deutsches Haus (German House). Close by is Wachenfeld House, a cosy wooden bungalow with simple guest rooms next to the Platterhof restaurant. Hitler intends to buy Wachenfeld House with the royalties from his book. While on parole, he is banned from speaking in any of the Prussian provinces and in Bavaria. The ban is to last for another two years.

Instead he writes political editorials for the *Völkische Beobachter*. His first article after his release from Landsberg prison is entitled 'A New Beginning'. He demands a high fee for his editorials, for they are his only means of income. One reason Hitler has chosen the Obersalzberg as a refuge is its proximity to the Austrian frontier; on a moment's notice, he can slip over the line and evade arrest by the German police. In his tax returns for 1924, Hitler lists his profession as 'writer'.

He attempts to justify a high proportion of his income as deductible expenses.

Hitler lives a quiet, almost domestic life in Berchtesgaden. At night, he wears brown slippers with a cutaway. His widowed half-sister who worked in Vienna as a housekeeper comes over to take care of her famous brother. She bakes wonderful Viennese pastries for which he has a ravenous appetite. She brings her blond, pretty, 17-year-old daughter Angela with her pleasant voice. Hitler shortens her name to 'Geli'. Geli has been attending singing classes in Vienna and has the ambition to become an opera singer. Occasionally Hitler returns to Munich, about 74 miles by train. In Munich he gobbles half a dozen chocolate cakes at the Carlton Tea Room and goes to the cinema twice a day. He gets rid of his walking stick and tops up his attire with a dog whip of hippopotamus hide. Hitler confidently plans to write a second book, which he titles *The Monumental History of Humanity*. For amusement, he goes on picnics.

When Hitler comes out of Landsberg prison, the inflation is over. Reparations payments have been scaled down. America is prepared to make loans to Germany. Since reparations payments turned out to be less than German borrowings, the United States themselves were financing their own compensation for war losses. The war debt has been 'paid off' in worthless paper money. Hjalmar Schacht (who in 1933 is appointed by Hitler to the presidency of the Reichsbank) is a private banker and middle-of-the-road politician who also happens to be a member of the June-Club. He has been appointed as a special commissioner to deal with the inflation problem. He has issued a new currency, the so-called

Rentenmark. One trillion of the old Reichmarks exchanges for one of Schacht's new Rentenmarks. The new currency is nominally backed by all of Germany's land and real estate. The French troops have left the Ruhr. A period of recovery has set in for Germany. Again there is money to be made. There is no shortage of chocolate, milk and beer.

In February 1925, the Munich Carnival is held for the first time since the outbreak of war in 1914. People are singing and dancing in the streets all night long when Weimar president Friedrich 'Fritz' Ebert, still only in his mid-50s, dies of a ruptured appendix; he had ignored doctor's orders to undergo an operation. A new president has to be elected. At the request of the Strasser brothers, General Ludendorff is put forward by the Nazi Party as its candidate. Hitler promises Ludendorff his full support. In the presidential election which follows, Ludendorff is heavily defeated. The general receives only slightly over 200,000 votes out of a total of nearly 28 million. The election is inconclusive, and a second round is held. Ludendorff withdraws. His old commander Paul von Hindenburg, the field marshal, a nationalist and a monarchist, appears as the candidate for the presidency of a coalition of the conservative right. Hindenburg is elected Reich President. He is 88 years of age. His mental and physical powers are waning; he is far too senile to fully realize what is happening. It is said that no bureaucrat dares to leave a sandwich paper near the President for fear that the old Hindenburg will mistake it for a state paper and sign it.

Hitler sets himself the task of re-creating his movement. He puts his bodyguards in black uniforms similar to those worn by the Italian Fascists and makes them swear an oath of loyalty to him personally. Hitler intends to mould his party into a military-style organization such as Germany has never seen before, not even under Bismarck or Frederick the Great.

While Hitler flexes his muscles, Moeller van den Bruck develops syphilis of the brain. Chronic and disabling, the disease invades his cardiovascular and nervous system. He has difficulty maintaining his balance. Sharp, stabbing pains in his legs force him to adopt a somewhat odd walk, with a wide base. He is confused about his own identity and starts impersonating Nietzsche, Edgar Allan Poe and Guy de Maupassant. He prepares himself a glass of laudanum, dissolving powdered opium in alcohol. Moeller van den Bruck is well aware that in Poe's time, a laudanum solution was administered through cotton earplugs to hallucinating patients in mental hospitals. The drug works quickly, producing maximum respiratory depression in 10 minutes, and its peak effect of relief from agony and raving attacks in less than 20 minutes. He tries to medicate his condition with even more alcohol. There are long, hideous nights of despair; in his delirium Moeller van den Bruck overhears some men plotting to kill him on a train. He imagines his mother being mutilated; her tormentors saw off her feet at the ankles, her legs to the knees, then saw off her thighs at the hips.

When he was 44, Nietzsche said to his mother he had been in a lunatic asylum but would be all right again as he was still young, only 22. Repeatedly, Nietzsche called himself the Duke of Cumberland or the Kaiser, and on one occasion he said that 'last time, he was Frederick Wilhelm IV', an imaginary king or emperor.

Moeller van den Bruck intermittently shakes hands with his doctor. He is confused and, in his own words, 'ill and depressed'. The doctor signs a statement diagnosing 'mental degeneration'. He is given ever more tranquillizing medication, a calmative sodium and chloral, the oily liquid that is used in psychotherapy as a hypnotic. Like Guy de Maupassant before him, Moeller van den Bruck crawls on the floor.

It is said that De Maupassant ate his own excrement; a contemporary hospital report reads: *'Monsieur de Maupassant s'animalise'* (Monsieur de Maupassant is becoming an animal). Guy de Maupassant finally slashed his throat.

Moeller van den Bruck glides into long, halcyon calms, peaceful and tranquil, in which he tries to write, but his sentences are cut off, the words meaningless. Hölderlin and Kleist have gone mad, too. Kleist shoots himself on Lake Wannsee. All the while, Moeller van den Bruck is grimacing. As his condition worsens, he stays in bed most of the day, or sits in an armchair facing the death-mask of Napoleon on black silk on the wall, situated between his books, the Beardsley drawings, the satanical Félicien Rops etchings and his Jan Toorop paintings. He complains of headaches on the right side of his head, but doesn't stop smiling all the time. Yet he is easily reduced to tears. For most of the day, Moeller van den Bruck is silent, staring for long times at his hands. When he opens his mouth, he endlessly repeats confused, insensible, muttering sentences.

Nietzsche was 46 when he succumbed to the horrors of syphilis, Guy de Maupassant 42, Edgar Allan Poe barely 40, Kleist was 44. Moeller van den Bruck is 49. The doctors put him in a strait-jacket and he is admitted to the Grünewalder Sanatorium, a mental asylum in the Luzerner-Strasse, near the Parkfriedhof Lichterfelde cemetery, in the same sunny, green district of Berlin-Steglitz where he has lived for the past 15 years, and where his close neighbours over the years have been Ernst Jünger, Franz Kafka, George Grosz, Rosa Luxemburg and Franz Mehring, the first German Karl Marx biographer.

In March 1925, Hitler and Hess are driven by Emil Maurice in Hitler's newly acquired 15/70/100 PS-Compressor-Mercedes to Berlin. Hitler calls his car 'my supercharged Mercedes'. Late snow covers the bridges across the River Spree. Hess has never been in Berlin before. They stay at the wonderful rococo-style house of the Bechstein piano manufacturers in the Johannis-Strasse, between the Friedrich-Strasse and the city centre. Hitler feels at ease here. There are old masters on the walls, and the floors are covered with oriental silk carpets. Upon arrival, Hitler is showered with presents. The next day, they visit the exhibition of artefacts of King Armenophobis IV in the new Egyptian Museum. In front of the museum, an array of sphinxes are aligned. Inside they admire the bust of Nefertiti from Tell el-Amarna on the Upper Nile, unearthed in 1912 by a team of German archaeologists. From the Egyptian Museum, Hitler and Hess drive to the Luna-Park in downtown Berlin, where expressionist sculptures are exhibited by Pechstein and Rudolf Belling. From the Luna-Park, their sightseeing trip goes to the Sanssouci Castle in Potsdam, the summer house of Frederick the Great, built after his own design. At night, they slowly drive through the snowy streets of Berlin, along the grand avenue of Unter den Linden, past the cathedral which has been newly built in a Roman Renaissance style, while they gaze at some of the most elegant older buildings as well as the recent additions, such as the huge national monument to Kaiser Wilhelm I, completed in 1897. The elaborate monument includes a 30-ft high equestrian figure finished in marble, bronze and stone. Their car is often photographed; it is a unique model, custom-made for Hitler only. The next day, the car is on the front pages of the daily newspapers.

At the editorial offices of Otto Strasser's *Berliner Arbeiterzeitung* Hitler discusses party tactics with the Strasser brothers and Joseph Goebbels. They arrange for Hitler's new Munich-based magazine, the *Illustrated Beobachter*, to be sold in Berlin by units of Storm Troopers marching up and down the high street. Otto Strasser informs Hitler that Moeller van den Bruck has been interned in a psychiatric hospital. Hitler is not interested. He denounces Moeller van den Bruck as a 'parlor Bolshevik' and 'a political boy-scout'.

'But you are mistaken, *Herr* Hitler,' Strasser says innocently.

'I cannot be mistaken!' Hitler exclaims in a fury. 'Everything I do and say is historical. Each party member has to obey only the Führer! Me!'

'No!' Strasser replies. 'What you say is all very well for the Roman Church from which, incidentally, Italian Fascism took its inspiration, but not for Germany.'

'We disagree!' Hitler barks. He sits down and begins rubbing his knees with a circular motion that grows faster and faster. 'Our organization is based on discipline,' Hitler declares. 'Those who rule must know that they have the right to rule because they belong to a superior race. The Aryan race has the right to dominate the world, and that right will be the guiding principle of our foreign policy.'

'But *Herr* Hitler,' tries Otto Strasser, 'one of the principal aims of German foreign policy will have to be the abolition of the Versailles Treaty.'

'Nobody is interested in your high ideals,' Hitler snarls. 'People want bread and games.'

Otto Strasser is instantly dismissed.

They all go the cinema to see *Ben Hur*, a two and a half hour silent epic. Emil Maurice stays with the car. Hitler enjoys *Ben Hur*, but Hess says it's a Jewish propaganda vehicle. 'A distortion of history,' he snaps. 'The Romans crucify Jesus while the good Jews try to prevent it from happening.'

Hitler has abandoned his alleged plan to appoint Gregor Strasser deputy leader of the Nazi Party. Hess sends a picture postcard of a Berlin landmark to his parents in Egypt, on the back of which he writes: 'I love this city, and now H[itler] adores it too. He dreams of adding new buildings to the imperial metropolis.'

As a symbol of the new, modern spirit, street advertisements are written in lower case. In the big, ugly city of Berlin the artist George Grosz makes a drawing of Christ on the cross in a gas mask, wearing army boots. He is prosecuted and fined for defaming the military, corrupting public morals and committing blasphemy. The literary event of the year is the publication of Thomas Mann's *The Magic Mountain*, a bulky two-volume novel. In its first year, it sells 50,000 copies. Hitler's half-brother Alois Matzelsberger, who has been a waiter at the Shelbourne Hotel in Liverpool while married to Bridget Dowling, is sentenced to six months in prison by a Hamburg court for bigamy. Released from prison, he comes to Berlin and opens a small beer house in a Berlin suburb; he then moves to the fashionable Wittenbergplatz to open a popular restaurant named Alois. Hitler's nephew Adolf Raubal is living modestly in a student hostel in Berlin. He makes some money on the side as an inventor at the technical college.

Storm Troopers are marching through the streets, shouting, 'Germany, wake up!' New customs have taken hold of the city: the weekend, and 5 o'clock tea. Berlin is surrounded by beautiful lakes and woods easily accessible by streetcar or bus. At the end of the bus line are beer gardens, dancehalls and amusement parks. City dwellers in need of fresh air, nature and solitude eat pickled cucumber at the Wannsee beach in a place called Lübbenau. The Femina night club displays pictures of smiling, almost naked young women on its billboards. During the intermission, pine scent is sprayed in the movie palaces. Hitler's *Völkische Beobachter* and the *Illustrated Beobachter* are sold all over Germany by Storm Troopers in shining boots wearing cartridge belts and automatic Luger pistols. In Berlin, ostrich riding is the gimmick of the day. A Nazi in uniform strolls into a shop. A Jewish boy runs off to the men's room. Everyone in the shop stands at attention.

In the Motz-Strasse where the few remaining members of the June-Club meet on Monday nights for intellectual discussion, a discreet night club has opened its doors where men dance with men and women with women. The club is called The Eldorado. Every night, customers get a prize for the most original dance costume: first prize a live monkey, second prize a live parrot. In an effort to erase the memory of Moeller van den Bruck, co-founder Heinrich von Gleichen takes over the leadership of the June-Club and renames it *Herren-Klub* (Men's Club). The Men's Club is located in the same offices and frequents the same tavern in the Motz-Strasse as the former June-Club. The novelist Hans Grimm who was one of the moral pillars of the June-Club immediately joins the Men's Club. 'If Hitler won't do it, no-one will do it,' Grimm says. The past is in ruins, the present shattered, the future is their only hope. Such is their conviction.

In the Behrens-Strasse, next to the Johannis-Strasse where the wealthy Bechsteins live, there is a new night club in every house, in every basement. On the elegant Kurfürstendamm a lesbian bar opens. The Tiller Girls dance in the street to advertise their show at the Scala Theatre. In the Invaliden-Strasse two dead horses are lying side by side on the footpath. They have accidentally been shot in some street fighting. With broken glass and pocket knives, passers-by carefully remove the hide; then they cut the corpses to pieces. 'I am fed up with eating turnips for years!' a woman shouts. Cocaine is sold in perfume bottles. Party speaker Joseph Goebbels christens Berlin 'a stone desert of sin, vice and corruption'. The war had been a release from boredom, but a renewed boredom seeps in. A world of which 'one is so tired, so dreadfully tired' is collapsing. But even the liberal art publisher Paul Cassirer describes the revolution as 'nothing but a great swindle'.

Berlin's middle-class apartments are designed not by architects but by the Imperial Prussian Police Department. One has to go through the bedroom and a long, narrow corridor to reach the kitchen. The result of poor housing is a high mortality rate and a zero population growth. Many Berliners have no home at all; they rent a bed by the hour. 'The revolution of stupidity is followed by the revolution of vulgarity,' says Oswald Spengler. He rejects the Weimar Republic in favour of a military dictatorship. A Jew conducts the Berlin Philharmonic.

Hitler surprisingly declares that 'the beer hall putsch of 1923 was a mistake, and I do not share the hostility of General Ludendorff towards the Catholic church either. The only aim of National Socialism is the defeat of Marxism. I will rise to power legally, within the framework of the constitution.' Privately Hitler confesses that he wants to get rid of Ludendorff as soon as possible. One of the art shops on Unter den Linden exhibits a large portrait of Adolf Hitler in its display window. With his slick dark hair, Hitler looks like a provincial dandy.

In cinemas all over the country, Storm Troopers are lining the aisles not to watch the film but to keep an eye on the spectators. General Ludendorff retires from active political life. He adheres to a new religion of sun-worshipping while his wife sponsors an anti-Masonic campaign. Hitler hands out postcard photographs of himself, inscribed with '*Heil* Hitler!' The journalist Kurt Tucholsky who writes satirical pieces for cabaret cries out: 'How can we avoid the next slaughter? *How? How?* He calls it a disgrace that 'the bowling-club chairmen of the political parties' do not have the moral courage to turn their back on Hitler's advertisements for war. 'Damn you. And bless you,' is the satirist's final remark. In the street, boys in brown flannel shirts are shooting because the noise of the bullets firing is fun. The Marxist philosopher Ernst Bloch says: 'Hitler, Hitlerism and Fascism are the ecstasy of the bourgeois youth.' A police superintendent in Berlin named Ernst Engelbrecht becomes the best-selling author of fictional books on urban crime. Véra and Vladimir Nabokov get married in Berlin on 15 April. The consumption of beer sausages at Aschinger's popular restaurant has gone up from 40,000 pairs per day to 65,000 pairs because of the confidence the old field marshal inspires as President.

From the Grünewald Sanatorium, Moeller van den Bruck releases his last political statement: 'I am immensely pleased by the Hindenburg election. It is a triumph of nationalism.' Through a sanatorium window, he waves farewell to his wife Lucy, and to his ex-wife Hedda, who have come to visit him one last time, for one last kiss. Some 25 years previously, still a very young man, Moeller van den Bruck has translated from English into German the following harsh statement which Thomas de Quincey had written in his *Confessions of an English Opium-Eater* in 1822: 'I will live no more mortal anguish and nervous terrors, the fear of death by brain fever or by lunacy.'

On 30 May 1925, Moeller van den Bruck collapses onto a stool, a revolver in his right hand. 'What do you intend to do with your revolver?' he asks himself. He does not respond. 'Is the revolver loaded?' He does not respond. 'Answer me, is the revolver loaded?' A powerful shot, a trickle of blood, and the room fills with gunsmoke. He has left a simple handwritten suicide note: '*Ich rette unsere Sache* (I die for our cause).' Moeller van den Bruck has come to his end with the adage of Heinrich von Kleist on his lips: *free in life, free in death.*

The hospital doctor records suicide. There is no post-mortem, and the prosecutor's office gives the go-ahead for the burial. Moeller van den Bruck is laid to rest in the Parkfriedhof Lichterfelde cemetery, among a long row of ordinary graves.

None of the Berlin newspapers publishes the customary obituary. Hans Schwarz, one of the influential members of the June-Club, pays his respects to the deceased in a moving last tribute: 'When the demons that darkened his spirit sought to down him, Moeller van den Bruck died a German death.' Hans Schwarz is chairman of countless party-owned companies. He will soon become State Treasurer of the Nazi Party. By now, the Romanisches Café is full of Nazis with intellectual aspirations. Instead of Billy Wilder or Joseph Roth, Ernst Jünger and Joseph Goebbels are drinking mocha in 'the swimming-pool'. Those who no longer want to be seen at the Romanisches Café go to Café Zunz on Tauentzien-Strasse down the block.

Nazi publisher Max Amann is disappointed in the contents of Hitler's book. He had hoped for an adventurous autobiography and a sensational eyewitness account, full of revelations of the beer hall putsch. What he gets is a crudely written, dull pseudo-philosophical treaty, filled with long words and awkward expressions, and with an impossible title. Amann is convinced that publishing the 400-page book is commercial suicide. He shortens the book's overlong title to *Mein Kampf* (My Struggle). The first edition of Hitler's self-portrait is published on 18 July 1925 with a first print run of 10,000 copies. It is priced at 12 marks, about double the price of most books, because Hitler wants to make money. The book includes an appendix which features posters advertising 27 meetings at which Hitler spoke.

In an author's preface, *Mein Kampf* is dedicated to the memory of the 16 'fallen heroes' who died 'at half past twelve on the afternoon of 9 November 1923 in the forecourt of the Feldherrnhalle in Munich'. The book ends with a loving tribute to Dietrich Eckart, the spiritual founder of National Socialism, who died in Landsberg prison of alcohol poisoning. Within a year, *Mein Kampf* has sold out and has to be reprinted.

Life goes on. When Max Beckmann starts to paint again, his baroque style has given way to a tortured, compact, cool expressionism, drab and devoid of beauty. There is no sentiment in Max Beckmann's work any more. In his paintings, the sun is blacked out. His human creatures are deformed by hunger, lust, disease, suffering, pain, loneliness. The painter has lived through hell. When evening comes, he wanders over the bridge and eats a meal in a bar where girls sit around and a jazz band plays neurotic tunes. Then he goes to the railway station restaurant. There he sits with a black cigar, drinking champagne, and looks straight ahead with blue eyes frozen in a pale, round face. His newest paintings are some of the most gruesome images ever painted. The diseases of war. Perhaps the desperate men and women clinging to the lifeboats in his *Sinking of the 'Titanic'* had not been survivors after all, but nothing more than the human pawns on the chessboard also known as the 'Great Spectacle of Life'.

Two men and a woman choose Berlin as a starting point for a walking trip. They set out from the Brandenburg Gate; they consider it will take them four and a half years to walk around the globe. The men wonder, 'What will Berlin look like by the time we get back?' In the middle of all the turmoil, the Kaiser-Wilhelm-Gedächtnis church opposite the Café Zinz and down the road from the Romanisches Café stretches its narrow steeples up into the grey evening twilight. Like an anachronism left behind, it mourns between the cafés and the cabarets, the cinemas and the cocaine dealers, and calmly, sadly announces the hour. In Munich the comedian Kurt Valentin rushes in front of the stage curtain, raises his right arm and yells: '*Heil* . . . dammit, now I forget his name!' The party is over, my friends. The party is over.

SIX

Epilogue

In a small apartment on the Düsseldorfer-Strasse in Munich, a man has no shoes or slippers on, just socks. Black, silk socks. 'I am so terribly dependent on my wife,' he moans. He slowly shuffles around the sunlit room, hands outstretched, as if he were going blind. 'Physically I am a human wreck,' he sighs, but my mind is as vital and as sharp as ever and I can still t–h–i–n–k, *mein Gott*!' His feet are small and elegant. He snorts, his nostrils flaring, and shouts, 'I can smell Hitler!'

For me, history is photographs in black and white. For him, history is memory. He is dressed as if he were a history photograph, in smart black trousers and a black silk shirt. A white silky scarf is tied around his bird-like neck. We are sitting in the warm afternoon sun. His hands and face are bedecked with dark liver spots. He coughs dangerously, spitting on the empty table. He produces a giant white handkerchief and wipes the table clean. Otto Strasser is the last surviving member of the original band of Nazi Party leaders. It is 1974 and he is 76 years of age. On 30 June 1934 his brother Gregor, who was five years his senior, was arrested by the Gestapo and killed by a rain of bullets fired through the bars of his prison cell.

'Hitler had my brother shot down like a sparrow,' Otto Strasser says, 'although he was godfather to Gregor's twin sons.' The following Sunday, his grieving widow received an urn filled with ashes, bearing the inscription: 'Gregor Strasser, died 30.VI.34, Secret State Police Office, Berlin'.

'*Ach*,' Otto Strasser murmurs, 'I knew Hitler so well. We met at the house of Gregor way back in 1921. Hitler looked rather funny with that fly under his nose. Not like a charismatic leader at all; more like a manservant. After our first meeting, I said to my mother: "Hitler is not a political animal or a future statesman; he is a faith healer." After Gregor and I had joined the party, Hitler often came to our house for lunch. He must have loved my mother's salad dishes. Mother compared Hitler to a circus clown.' He moans, spits and snorts. 'A circus clown? One who killed my brother and stole a revolutionary idea equal to *Das Kapital* and *The Origin of Species* from under the nose of one of my best friends. Without Hitler, Moeller van den Bruck would have become a household name, on a par with Marx and Charles Darwin.' Otto Strasser shakes his old and rumpled head. The large duelling scar on his left cheek has become almost invisible, sunken as it is in the deep lines of his hollow face. Death is etched all over him. His eyes fill with tears. He starts sobbing, quietly, silently, and tears thick as blood run down his cheeks.

'Moeller van den Bruck took his life on the day he realized that Hitler was betraying his ideal,' Otto Strasser says. 'Hitler, of course, had borrowed the title of Moeller van den Bruck's book for his own use. People tend to ignore it today, but up to 1930 *The Third Reich* was widely read and discussed in Germany, much more so than *Mein Kampf*. A Nazi reprint was issued, and in fact, *The Third Reich* not *Mein Kampf* was the bible of Nazi ideology. By 1933, less than 10 years after Moeller van den Bruck committed suicide, 130,000 copies of *The Third Reich* had been sold. This got on Hitler's nerves and he ordered Alfred Rosenberg to start a smear campaign in the *Völkische Beobachter* against Moeller van den Bruck. Goebbels followed suit and shrieked that Moeller van den Bruck had stolen his ideas from Hitler. Goebbels was a cynical, calculating seducer. While Hitler was devoid of morals, because he did not know what morals are, Goebbels was immoral because although he knew how to behave morally he chose to act otherwise. Acting upon his orders, the Storm Troopers stepped in. Lucy and Moeller van den Bruck's home was raided and his library plundered. His private papers and all of his letters and manuscripts were confiscated. They were stored in the Nazi Archive in one of the rooms of the Bauakademie (Building Academy) in the Dorotheen-Strasse in Berlin.'

'That wasn't the end of it. On 10 May 1933, students and Storm Troopers invaded public and private libraries and collected the books by Jewish, Marxist, Bolshevist and other disruptive authors and publicly burned them in huge bonfires in front of Berlin University: books by non-German authors, dead and alive, such as Emile Zola, Marcel Proust, Jack London, H.G. Wells, Sigmund Freud, Upton Sinclair and Franz Kafka, but also by the German authors Thomas Mann, Erich Maria Remarque and Moeller van den Bruck. His name had to be erased from the consciousness of the German people because Hitler was the visionary, not a mentally unstable dandy and a despised intellectual who shot himself in a mental asylum. Joseph Goebbels made a short speech after the book burning: "Spirits are awakening, oh century. It is a joy to live!" With *The Third Reich* out of the way, Adolf Hitler's *Mein Kampf* was promoted as the highest form of literary art.'

A school text advertises *Mein Kampf* as 'a classic masterpiece' and 'the new Bible of the People'. Booksellers are only allowed to deal in new copies, since the literary work of the Führer cannot be described as 'second-hand'. Already in 1925, the literary agency of Curtis Brown in London, with offices in Berlin, enters into copyright negotiations. An advance on royalties of £350 is paid to Eher-Verlag, the Nazi publishing house. In London, negotiations are conducted with Dr Hans Wilhelm Thost, the official London correspondent of Eher-Verlag. He is later expelled on suspicion of espionage. In 1932, the Hearst syndicate offers $25,000 for the American translation rights. On 29 July 1933, Houghton, Mifflin & Co. of Boston contact Eher-Verlag with an offer to 'manufacture and publish' *Mein Kampf* for sale in book form. As a result, the first foreign-language edition of Hitler's book is published in the United States in 1933 as *My Battle*. Simultaneously it is published in Britain under the imprint of Hurst & Blackett, a subsidiary of the Hutchinson publishing group. In Britain, Hitler's title is rendered as *My Struggle*. The English edition includes the unabridged text of the Nazi Party programme.

Although *Manchester Guardian* correspondent Robert Dell, who understands Nazi policy, finds it 'difficult to avoid the conclusion that the publication of the translation is an attempt to dupe the English-speaking public, since all the passages likely to make a bad impression have been omitted', *The Times* prints four extracts. *The Bookseller*, the trade journal, attests: 'The text runs to 560 pages of close print, yet it was set up in type in four working days, and the book was printed in four days. The translator worked night and day during that period, sending proofs back in batches by taxi.' The publisher refuses to reveal the identity of the translator.

Two years after its first British publication, a Paternoster Library edition with reduced format and without the illustrations is published. Combined sales of both British editions total 47,000 copies by August 1938. Copies of Hitler's *My Struggle*, as well as of Karl Marx's *Das Kapital*, are among the books officially recommended as gifts to British troops at the war front in 1939. By September 1940, the total number of copies sold in the United States is approximately 100,000.

An *Honorar-Buch*, the publisher's and author's royalties ledger, is confiscated from German archives at the end of the Second World War and is now in the Library of Congress in Washington, DC. It confirms Otto Strasser's later assumption that *Mein Kampf* isn't that widely read in the late 1920s: German sales slump to 6,913 copies in 1926, 5,607 in 1927, and only 3,015 copies in 1928. Then sales go up again: 7,664 copies are sold in 1929. The next year, an inexpensive edition is published at a price of 8 marks. It sells 54,084 copies in 1930, slightly less in 1931 and an impressive 90,351 in 1932. In 1933, President Hindenburg entrusts the chancellorship to Adolf Hitler. In Hitler's first year in high office, *Mein Kampf* sells 1 million copies. The author's royalties, which have been increased from 10 to 15 per cent after 1 January 1933, are over 1 million marks, making Hitler a first-time millionaire and the most prosperous literary author in Nazi Germany. Every German couple about to be married is expected to buy the book. Hitler's fiftieth birthday in April 1939, coinciding with the sale of the 5-millionth copy of *Mein Kampf,* is marked by the publication of a deluxe edition, bound in dark blue leather, decorated in gold, with the upthrust naked blade of a sword displayed on the cover.

Soon authorized translations are published in the Scandinavian languages, in Czech (*Muj Boy*), Dutch (*Mijn Kamp*), Italian (*La Mia Vita*), Spanish (*Mi Lucha*), Portuguese (*Minha Luta*), Hungarian (*Harcóm*) and Russian. The Russian edition, entitled *Adolf Hitler: Moya Borba. Avtobiografiya,* is printed in Shangai where Lieutenant-Colonel Kriebel, who has been with Hitler in Landsberg prison, is appointed consul on the day Hitler becomes Chancellor of the Reich. Japanese, Arabic and Tamil translations follow. Among the personal possessions of Egyptians captured by the Israelis during the Sinai occupation in November 1956 are 'kitbag editions' of *Mein Kampf* published by the Beirut Printing and Publishing House. Hebrew University in Jerusalem bring out the first Hebrew translation of *Mein Kampf* in 1995 under the title *Maawaki.*

Shortly after the book has been publicly burned in the cruel bonfire on the courtyard in front of Berlin University, Moeller van den Bruck's *The Third Reich* is published in English by the company of George Allen & Unwin in Museum Street, in a condensed, 'authorized' translation by E.O. Lorimer. Amazingly, the translator has retitled the book *Germany's Third Empire.* In its foreword, it is labelled 'a message to Moeller van den Bruck's fellow countrymen'. 'Magnificent book!' exclaims the *Listener.* The *Manchester Guardian* reviews the book as 'a work of true genius' and reaches the conclusion that it is 'worthy of ranking beside some of

Nietzsche's finest writings'. Yet, the English translation of *The Third Reich* sinks without trace. Two copies are preserved in the British Library.

In an attempt to find out what has happened to the Moeller van den Bruck archive stored on Hitler's orders in the Bauakademie building in Berlin, I went to see Otto Günsche and Dr Werner Naumann. While Günsche had been Hitler's last SS bodyguard, Dr Naumann served as Secretary of State in Goebbels's Propaganda Ministry in the final days of the Third Reich. After the war, both became captains of industry in the prosperous Rhineland. This is the story they told me, and which I recorded:

Berlin, April 1945. Adolf Hitler has become an old man who has lost his strength, and his will to live and to fight. Otto Günsche, his personal bodyguard, stands at attention at the door of the ante-room leading to Hitler's private suite in the Führerbunker. The previous day, Hitler married Eva Braun. There has been no big party, just a glass of champagne and some smiles. Hitler extends his hand. Günsche shakes the hand of his Führer and says: 'Good night, *mein Chef!*' Although it is early afternoon, he is of the opinion that Hitler and Eva Braun are preparing to go to bed. In the underground bunker, day and night have blended into one grey mass of time. Hitler is dressed in a uniform jacket and black trousers. He is wearing black gloves too, and his Iron Cross. He smiles and says to Günsche: 'Fräulein Braun and I are going to depart this life. I want you to burn our bodies. I do not want my body to be displayed in a Russian freak show!' '*Jawohl, mein Chef,*' the bodyguard answers. Before retreating to his private rooms, Hitler turns around and adds: 'For me, death only means freedom from worries and from a very difficult life. But you, *you* must break out. You must live!'

A Russian ground attack on the bunker is imminent. Berlin is engulfed in a sea of flames. At any moment, Russian troops can storm the Chancellery. Very calm and in a relaxed, almost cheerful manner Hitler retreats to his private rooms. By phone Günsche orders Hitler's chauffeur to fetch some petrol. Then he takes up position outside Hitler's door again. He has received orders not to let anyone in. Joseph Goebbels is in the room opposite the antechamber to Hitler's private rooms which he uses as his office. It is extremely noisy in the bunker – which is two storeys deep – with the whirling of the ventilators and the throbbing of the diesel engines in the machine room. Yet a quiet peace descends over all those in the bunker, as the wait for Hitler's death begins. Then, the dull sound of one single shot. Hitler sits in his armchair. He has a gunshot injury to his head above the right eyelid. There are some bloodstains on the sofa, and some spots of blood on the wall. Blood is also dripping onto the carpet. Hitler is 56 years of age, exactly the same age as the Holy Roman Emperor Frederick II when he died. A flower vase has fallen over, staining two more items prominently displayed on the table: a clumsy pen-and-ink drawing of the Comines church tower in ruins, dated 1918, and a copy of the 1923 edition of *The Third Reich* opened at its title page. The book is inscribed 'To Adolf Hitler' and signed 'Moeller van den Bruck'.

Günsche looks at his wristwatch. It is 1530 hours exactly, on 30 April 1945. He picks up the vase and puts it upright again. He does not touch the book or the drawing. Hitler's eyes are wide open. Eva Braun's eyes are open too. She wears Hitler's favourite dress, black with pink roses on either side of a low, square neckline. One cyanide capsule that looks like an empty lipstick tube lies on the floor. Günsche moves to the briefing room where Martin Bormann, Joseph Goebbels, the generals Krebs and Burgdorf and Goebbels's state secretary Dr Werner Naumann are waiting for news, and reports: 'The Führer is dead.' With the help of Martin Bormann, Günsche drapes the bodies of Hitler and Eva Braun in a silk Persian carpet and carries them to the ruined garden of the Chancellery. Soviet howitzers, rocket launchers and Stalin organs open fire. Shells explode incessantly, and gunfire thunders through the canyons of rubble.

The bodies are placed in a shallow bomb crater and Günsche pours petrol over them. Russian shells are falling, the sky is illuminated by flares. Günsche wants to blow up the bodies with a hand grenade, but Bormann lights some telegrams that are lying around and tries to set the bodies on fire with a paper fuse. Günsche pours some more petrol, dips a rag in it, sets it alight and throws the rag upon the corpses. A whoosh and the two bodies catch fire. Black smoke rises into the foul air. Side by side, Bormann and Günsche raise their arm in a final Nazi salute over the burning bodies that are engulfed in flames, until the charred and shrunken corpses are no longer identifiable. Then they hurry back underground.

Russian troops are storming into the streets next to the Chancellery. If the Nazis trapped in the bunker want to get out, they will have to work their way through 2½ million *soldateska* who cover the Berlin area. The Russians know no mercy. They have heard radio broadcasts that Hitler is still in Berlin, and they fire on everything that moves. The last survivors of Hitler's court are told to be prepared for a mass escape through the Russian lines in the darkness of the night. First, they have to get out of the Führerbunker. Then they will have to run to the underground entrance at the Hotel Kaiserhof and move as far as they can in the meandering tunnels under the ruined city until they reach a spot where they can emerge safely.

'The objective is the River Spree,' Bormann says. 'As far as we know, the Russians haven't reached Charlottenburg.' Then he shouts, 'Every man for himself!' The generals Krebs and Burgdorf are sitting at a long table covered with glasses and empty bottles. Almost unconscious from too much brandy, they shoot themselves; 25-year-old Constanze Manziarly, who has a small kitchen in the upper bunker where she prepared Hitler's vegetarian meals, takes her own life with prussic acid. Joseph Goebbels and his wife follow Hitler into death by committing suicide. Their six children in their long white nightgowns have died in their sleep from a lethal injection with a powerful soporific drug. Hitler's favourite dog Blondi has been killed in the same way.

The exodus is organized in several groups. Each group files safely through the vaults and tunnels and along the railway track. The first group with Bormann, Günsche and Dr Naumann reaches the Friedrich-Strasse surface up the ordinary stairway to the street. They step into an inferno. Rows of German tanks are rolling onto the railroad bridge. Bormann hides behind the lead tank, closely followed by Dr Naumann. The deafening sound of explosions, guns firing, shouting, and maximum-intensity fire fills the night air, thick with brick dust and smoke. Bormann is frightened; he has never been under fire before. Although the flash of an explosion temporarily blinds Dr Naumann, he sees Bormann, who was Hitler's private secretary, thrown into the air. Then Bormann is lying on his back, his limp body illuminated by the moonlight and a thousand fires from a doomed Berlin. Dr Naumann jumps, runs, and vanishes. The dark dawn is illuminated by the flaming of the burning city. Thousands of corpses are littering the ruins of the once mighty metropolis. Outside the post office in the Lehrter station, dead bodies are piled up. Mist from the river covers the ground.

In the nearby Tiergarten Zoo where Schliemann's Treasure of Troy is stored in an anti-aircraft tower, the trees are coming into bloom. Only a few animals are left alive in the zoo: the male elephant, a chimpanzee, a few small monkeys and a handful of tropical birds. A hippopotamus floats in its pool, the metal fins of an unexploded shell sticking out of its bloated body. Pongo, the biggest gorilla in Europe, is lying dead in his cage.

Battered buildings loom large through the morning mist. The Bauakademie building is reduced to rubble, and fire is destroying the Nazi Archive. The last remnants of Moeller van den Bruck's literary and political dream of an everlasting Third Reich go up in the smoke and flames of the bonfire of war. Meanwhile, the Russians have entered the Führerbunker. War correspondent Constantin Simonov who works for the *Pravda* newspaper enters Hitler's private quarters and snatches the Comines church drawing and the dedicated copy of *The Third Reich* from the wet tablecloth. The sketch turns out not to be a Hitler drawing of war devastation in Flanders fields; it is attributed to an unknown war artist. Russian soldiers sing and dance in the streets, and roast an African ox from the

Tiergarten Zoo while the poet Dolmatovsky recites patriotic verse. Early in the afternoon it starts raining.

A few books only, and an old black telephone. 'I warned my brother,' Otto Strasser groans. 'I said to him, "Watch out! Hitler is getting too powerful!" But Gregor didn't listen to me. He tried to soothe me. "Hitler is just a tribune," he said, "a drummer for support. Nothing to worry about. When we don't need him any more, we'll get rid of him."' Gregor obviously hadn't seen what I had seen, namely that Hitler was forever studying the hierachy of the Jesuit organization. He endlessly repeated that the Jesuits owe their leader blind obedience. The principle of leadership – to be responsible to those above and to be master to those below – had been adopted by Hitler. As an expert in political economy, I opposed that doctrine. Foreign diplomats have testified that when in a rage, Hitler rolled on the floor and chewed on the carpet. I've never seen him behave in this manner. But it certainly was not healthy to get too close to Hitler.

'His niece Geli Raubal killed herself with Hitler's pistol in the bedroom of his apartment in Munich after Hitler had found out she was having an affair with Emil Maurice, his butler and bodyguard whom he trusted above all, and a murder squad shot down Captain Röhm who was his best friend. The geopolitics professor Karl Haushofer was arrested on Hitler's orders and hanged on a piano wire. Father Bernhard Staempfle, who edited *Mein Kampf*, was found in a forest with his throat cut open and three bullets in his heart. Hitler despised everyone. My brother had sold his pharmacy to finance our daily and weekly Berlin papers, but Hitler ordered us to hand them over to Max

Amann's Eher-Verlag. I refused. Instead I created a new anti-Hitler party and called it Black Front. From that day on, my days were numbered. When Hitler became Chancellor, I fled the country and escaped into exile. Under an assumed name I lived first in Prague, then in Switzerland and Canada where I became an informant to the Intelligence Service. Goebbels proclaimed that I was Hitler's enemy No. 1.' Strasser coughs, his whole body shakes violently, as if he is about to explode. His silk handkerchief, no longer white, is drenched in blood and sputum. I should stop this conversation. '*Nein! Nein!*' Otto Strasser exclaims. 'As long as I live, I shall speak!' The next morning, 27 August 1974, on a lovely summer day, the last man alive who had known Moeller van den Bruck personally and intimately, died in Munich.

Bibliography

Adam, Reinhard, *Moeller van den Bruck* (Königsberg, Gräfe und Unzer, 1933).

Bach, Steven, *Marlene Dietrich. Life of a Legend* (London, Harper Collins, 1992).

Beckmann, Max, *Self-Portrait in Words* (University of Chicago Press, 1997).

Brian, Denis, *Einstein. A Life* (New York, John Wiley, 1996).

Bromberg, N. and Small, V., *Hitler's Psychopathology* (New York, Int. University Press, 1983).

Broszat, Martin, *Hitler and the collapse of Weimar Germany* (New York, Berg, 1983).

Bullock, A., *Hitler, A Study of Tyranny* (London, Oldhams Books, 1952).

Defoe, Daniel, *Moll Flanders* (London, Penguin Books, 1994).

De Quincey, Thomas, *Confessions of an English Opium-Eater* (London, Penguin Books, 1997).

Eberle, Matthias, *World War I and the Weimar artists* (New Haven/London, Yale University Press, 1985).

Eckardt, Wolf von and Gilman, Sander L., *Bertolt Brecht's Berlin* (London, Abelard, 1975).

Feuchtwanger, E.J., *From Weimar to Hitler* (London, Macmillan, 1993).

Field, Geoffrey G., *Evangelist of Race. The Germanic vision of Houston Stewart Chamberlain* (New York, Columbia University Press, 1981).

Friedrich, Thomas, *Berlin. A photographic portrait of the Weimar years*, foreword Stephen Spender (London, Tauris, 1991).

Gay, Peter, *Weimar Culture* (London, Secker & Warburg, 1968).

Hamann, Brigitte, *Hitlers Wien* (Munich, Piper, 1996).

Hamilton, Alastair, *The Appeal of Fascism* (London, Anthony Blond, 1971).

Hayman, Ronald, *Nietzsche. A critical Life* (London, Weidenfeld & Nicolson, 1970).

Heller, Reinhold, *Munch. His Life and Work* (London, John Murray, 1984).

Hess, Rudolf, *Briefe 1908–1933* (Munich, Langen-Müller, 1987).

Jarman, T.L., *The Rise and Fall of Nazi Germany* (New York, New American Library, 1961).

Jones, Sydney J., *Hitler in Vienna* (London, Blond & Briggs, 1988).

Kaes, A., Jay, M. and Dimendberg, E., *The Weimar Republic Sourcebook* (Berkeley, University of California Press, 1994).

Kafka, Franz, *Letters to Felice* (London, Penguin Books, 1978).

Kleemann, Elisabeth, *Zwischen symbolischen Rebellion und politischer Revolution* (Frankfurt am Main, Peter Lang, 1985).

Kurtz, Harold, *The Second Reich. Kaiser Wilhelm and his Germany* (London, Macdonald, 1970).

Langer, Walter C., *The Mind of Adolf Hitler. The Secret Wartime Report* (New York, Basic Books, 1972).

Laqueur, Walter, *Weimar. A cultural history 1918–1933* (London, Weidenfeld & Nicolson, 1974).

Launay, Jacques de, *Hitler en Belgique* (Strombeek-Bever, Byblos, 1975).

Lurfer, Otto, *Hitler hinter Heftungsmauern* (Berlin, E.S. Mittler & Sohn, 1933).

Manvell, R. and Fraenkel, H., *Doctor Goebbels. His Life and Death* (New York, Simon & Schuster, 1960).

——, *Hess* (London, Mac Gibbon & Kee, 1971).

Maugham, Somerset W., *The Moon and Sixpence* (New York, Grosset & Dunlap, 1919).

Mohler, Armin, *Die konservative Revolution in Deutschland, 1918–1932. Ein Handbuch* (Darmstadt, Wissenschaftliche Buchgesellschaft, 1972).

Mommsen, Wolfgang J., *Imperial Germany 1867–1918* (London/ New York, Arnold, 1995).

Morton, R.S., *Venereal Diseases* (London, Penguin, 1966).

Paris, Barry, *Garbo. A biography* (London, Sidgwick & Jackson, 1995).

Rabitsch, Hugo, *Aus Adolf Hitlers Jugendzeit* (Munich, Deutscher Volksverlag, 1933).

Roters, Eberhard, *Berlin 1910–1933* (New Jersey, Wellfleet Press, 1982).

Schack, Herbert, *Denker und Deuter. Männer von der deutsche Wende* (Stuttgart, Kröner, 1938).

Schrader, Bärbel and Schebera, Jürgen, *The Golden Twenties. Art and Literature in the Weimar Republic* (New Haven, Yale University Press, 1988).

Schwarzwäller, Wulf, *Rudolf Hess. The Deputy* (London, Quartet Books, 1988).

Schwierskott, Hans-Joachim, *Arthur Moeller van den Bruck und der revolutionäre Nationalismus in der Weimarer Republik* (Göttingen, Musterschmidt, 1962).

Shirer, William L., *The Rise and Fall of the Third Reich* (New York, Simon & Schuster, 1990).

Snyder, Louis L., *Encyclopedia of the Third Reich* (New York, McGraw-Hill, 1976).

Spoto, Donald, *Dietrich* (New York, Bantam Press, 1992).

Stachura, Peter D., *Gregor Strasser and the Rise of Nazism* (London, George Allen & Unwin, 1983).

Standinger, Hans, *The Inner Nazi* (Louisiana State University Press, 1981).

Strasser, Otto, *Hitler and I* (London, Jonathan Cape, 1940).

Tuchmann, Barbara W., *August 1914* (London, Constable, 1962).

Voss, Karl, *Reiseführer für Literaturfreunde Berlin* (Berlin, Ullstein, 1986).

Index